THE

5 EFFORTLESS HABITS TO
EXPAND YOUR COMFORT ZONE

RELUCTANT
CREATIVE

DR. CAROLINE BROOKFIELD

Artful
Science

D — DAYDREAM

A — AMBIGUITY

N — NOVELTY

C — CURIOSITY

E — EDIT LATER

Contents

Taking
THE CREATIVE LEAP

It was springtime in Toronto. I had just taken an elevator to the roof of the skyscraper. I left the elevator at the 86th floor and stepped out onto the narrow wooden plank. The rough and knotty board gently bobbed up and down in the inevitable gusts of wind, high above the road below. There was nowhere else to go. I looked down. The people below scuttled about like ants. I could hear faint horns and construction noises in the distance. A woman in the next building lounged in her window seat in flannel pajamas, reading a book, completely oblivious to my precarious position.

I carefully walked along the plank, to the sound of clanging bells — the warning bells in my mind. Sweat smeared my palms. My mouth felt dry. Jaw clenched. I knew I was safe, but everything in my body and brain were screaming at me to stop. Yet, I persevered and kept walking. Finally, at the end of the plank, I took a shaky but deep breath. I glanced at the woman in the window, secretly willing her to look my way, to force me to stop. She was too absorbed in her book to notice. I took another deep breath, looked down, and jumped.

As I fell, I flew past the neighbouring buildings, getting a glimpse of their lives through small windows to a million stories. About halfway down, I looked at the ground. Terror and curiosity filled my chest in equal measure. I could feel the pounding of my heart in my eardrums. 29, 20, 15, finally three floors to go, and I couldn't look. At the last second, I looked up to see the blue sky right before the impact blackened my sight.

"Holy s*#t! I can't believe she jumped!" I pulled off my headset and grinned at my small audience, feeling conflicted about my emotions — fear, pride, confusion, exhilaration and sadness, coursing through my body.

(You had to know this was virtual reality, right? I mean I did write this book, so either I survived a fall from 86 floors, or it wasn't real.)

Here's what happened. In February of 2020, we celebrated my son's 12th birthday at a Virtual Reality Arcade.

After the kids chased each other in their VR World, they happily stuffed their faces with cake in the Party Room, awaiting the moms for pick up. As each mom arrived, the VR manager offered to let them try out the plank game.

One after another, the moms put on the VR headset and rode the virtual elevator to the top floor. The first mom couldn't leave the elevator. The second mom left the elevator, put one foot on the plank, and gave up. I went next, and you know what happened. The fourth mom really, really wanted to walk the plank, but she couldn't override her survival instincts. Frustrated, she got down on her hands and knees and crawled carefully onto the plank. Tension radiated from her body like waves of heat. She crawled with a clenched jaw across the cheaply carpeted floor in the basement of a strip mall, terrified. Reaching her objective, the end of the plank, she victoriously removed the headset and exhaled slowly. With eyes as big as saucers, she proclaimed quietly, "that was intense." The last mom walked onto the plank. Slowly but surely, she got to the plank's end perched above the city and decided to quit while she was ahead. She did it! Her face was radiant as she ripped off the headset. By walking five steps across the floor, she had conquered climbing her own Mount Everest.

We all pushed our boundaries that day. Challenging the edge of our comfort zone is what gives us that thrill — that "Seeker's High" and the satisfaction and confidence to do it again. Jumping off the plank is not the end goal. Solving problems with our big brain, while managing deeply ingrained instincts to seek certainty and comfort provides the high of the challenge.

Our adult relationship with our creativity is like walking the virtual plank. We really want to step out, into uncertainty, over the abyss. We know it will be thrilling, daring, and satisfying to triumph over our senses. Logically, we know we're safe. We are in a basement, in a cubicle, in a strip mall. We know this. Yet, body and mind conspire together to keep us "safe."

Conform, fit in, don't be weird. Stay in your box that society has created for you, don't make waves. If everyone sits comfortably in their corporate-issued boxes, we feel safe, a bunch of box-sitters, conforming to artificial expectations of our behaviour. Yet, other box-sitters are desperately seeking an escape, and looking for permission to show some personal expression, maybe not to escape the box altogether but to decorate it, at least. It's like a game of chicken, only instead of street racers competing to see who will brake first in front of an obstacle, we're all sitting in company issued cardboard boxes, waiting to see who will crack first.

I'll tell you a little secret. I did something on the virtual plank that none of the other moms did. This small trick, when applied to your life, will give you the confidence to take bold, courageous action without perilous recklessness.

Fun Fact

I like the word **peril**, and I'm not going to apologize for using it frequently in this book. Some words are just fun to use. Do you have a favourite word? Scribble it in the margin! Go ahead! Well, if you are reading this on your computer, you can scribble it on your hand. Use this book to start challenging norms — you can write in this book; in fact I wish you would. If you hate the word peril, cross it out (in pen!!) and write in a word you prefer. I've left some hidden perilous treasures throughout the book, see if you can find all of the times I say some variation of "peril."

What's a word you love to use? Why?

_____

_____

When I stepped onto the plank, I was just as terrified as the other moms, even though I knew it was only Virtual Reality. Correction, a small part of my brain knew it was fake, the rest of me was freaking out. So, I used my big brain to create a test. On the plank, I remembered how to be a one-legged tree from my yoga training. Shifting my weight to my right foot (my good one), I slid my left foot out to the edge of the plank. I strained on my right leg, expecting that my left foot would touch air. At that critical moment, my toe touched cheap indoor carpeting. My brain instantly connected the dots — and they didn't add up. By integrating my senses, I *proved* that I was safe. Only in this moment did I gain the confidence to walk to the end of the plank and jump with a mix of exhilaration and trepidation. This was everyday creativity, paired with objective risk mitigation in action. Combining everyday creativity with objective risk mitigation is the basis of how to expand your comfort zone. Start to take more chances, try new things, and begin to buffer yourself against the fear of judgement of others that is holding you back from what you want to do.

In this book, I am going to help you to dance at the edge of your comfort zone.

D.A.N.C.E. is an acronym for five easy habits you can do in a few minutes a day to courageously welcome your creativity into your life. Creativity can feel dangerous, to step out over a virtual city and share your unique, deeply personal perspective with the world. With **D.A.N.C.E.**, you'll learn how to test your personal plank, to differentiate real danger from false danger, and to prove to your misfiring instincts that you are safe.

Think you aren't creative? Then why did you pick up this book? Clearly you think you are capable of creativity or want to incorporate it into your life. You are in good company — Ipsos asked lots of people about being creative. Of the 25% of people who were not creative, most either had not found the right activity, or just didn't know what to do. The good news, as I will outline in the following chapters, is that if you think you are too "left-brained" or analytical to be creative, science proves you wrong. Isn't that ironic?

Unlike rain on your wedding day, or a free ride when you've already paid. Those just kind of suck, but I guess it is also ironic that they are used in a song about irony[1].

As a veterinarian with a background in biomedical research, I can relate to the desire for data, a rubric, a checklist, or a linear progression to learn a new skill. But, as someone with ADHD (Attention Deficit Hyperactivity Disorder), I also have little patience for boring and complicated instructions, so I have tried to keep it simple. And that is why we **D.A.N.C.E.** to start finding our creative habits.

You can do one of the habits; you can do them all; you can even do them back to front. As Dr. Seuss *might* have said,

You can dance in the can, with a fan, or in a frying pan.
You may dance with a man, with a tan,
you can even dance while riding in a van.
Come on, act like Peter Pan, and create a fantastic plan,
you can even dance in Japan or Sudan.
And remember, this is where it all began.

Scribble your own Dr. Seuss rhyme in the margins (or on your hand). Try to write the rhyme at first without searching Google for "words that rhyme with plan."

---

1 Shoutout to '90s icon, Alanis Morrisette and irony with her iconic song, *Ironic*.
Listen right here for your nostalgia...and to see, was she really being ironic? Find the clip at thereluctantcreative.com/resources

These **D.A.N.C.E.** habits are based on research and experience, which I have applied to my own life, and with business leaders, moms, HR and insurance executives, entrepreneurs, pharmacy technicians, veterinarians, and more. Over the past three years, I have engaged with thought leaders on the future of work, creativity, and creative problem solving in organizations. Over the past 24 years as a veterinarian and researcher, I have prioritized the importance of data to guide creative solutions. I also believe in intellectual humility, to realize that we don't always know what we think we know, and that life's too short to have no fun. And for the past 48+ years I have been using and practising my own creativity, even though I can't draw a stick person or sing "*Happy Birthday!*" It's the secret sauce we all need this decade to survive the blasting sandstorms of change. Luckily, you already have it.

Choosing Science, Art, or the Knife's Edge

I was not always in love with creativity. Like most children, I loved to play and create. From a young age, because of my early love of animals, I knew I would become a veterinarian. A foregone conclusion, so I thought, until I reached high school. I surprised myself with a sudden love of improv, acting, stage makeup, and photography. I had never considered myself "artistic," but performance was a creative practice that made my heart sing. I was torn. I felt like I was standing on the knife edge of a high mountain, with art on one side and science on the other. I had to choose my path down. Since I didn't think I had the talent to live off my acting skills — and I had no idea how to become a cinematographer — the path to veterinary medicine was more defined. This, too, might sound familiar to you. On the fast track to preparing for a "successful" career, did you lose the time for Drama club, sketching in the park, or jamming with your friends? There was just so much *information* to absorb, memorize, and regurgitate. Newsflash, you know we have computers now that can remember it for us, with more accuracy now, right? I could never fathom, even in the 1980's, why I should memorize the Kreb's Cycle. If I was in a job requiring intimate knowledge of the Kreb's Cycle, I reasoned, I'm sure I could have it in a book nearby, and eventually I would learn it... because it was relevant to my life. Today, I try not to show my irritation when my kids report the random facts they are required to memorize, as if this is really the best use of their time and the precious real estate in their blossoming brains. I much prefer to see them tackling holistic projects like an art project using math principles, or a research project on solubility using everyday items.

Fast forward to a decade after vet school graduation, I felt a little stuck. I was competent in my field but felt an unsettling ennui. I sought variety in my profession to scratch that itch, but I could not quite reach it. The ennui remained.

Have you ever thought "is this it? Is this all there is?" Sure, you may enjoy your job, but do you ever feel like it should feel better? Or, if you're like me, have you hopped around to different positions, companies, and still not found the satisfaction you seek? Did you expect that the ease of accomplishment would help you feel like you arrived somewhere? Where are the deck chairs and pina coladas of success?

Every day, I am challenged as a veterinarian with the diversity of cases and the unpredictability of working with living organisms (and their pets). It wasn't until I created my first business that I found the missing piece. Building a website, developing products and services, and designing brochures and newsletters helped me to reconnect with my creativity. I thrived in learning new skills, and I loved the independence of prioritizing projects, being in control of my time, and risking failure. Over the following years, I exercised my creativity in untraditional ways, like public speaking in my role as a technical services veterinarian, writing a manual for wildlife rehabilitators, surgery on wild raptors and birds, and creative accounting in my role managing a 1-million-dollar research contract (just kidding… about the creative accounting bit, anyway.). Becoming a parent challenged my creativity with how to manage constraints, little dictators, and new ways of sneaking vegetables in food. To find a creative way to stay home with my kids, I built an online employment matching service for veterinarians. I loved building the website, choosing the fonts, connecting with partners, and helping veterinarians find the help they needed. I learned that I loved to create, but operations were a bit drearier. I also learned that sometimes there is a reason there is no competition in a space, as veterinarians struggled to get on board with the business model. They preferred to spend 25-hours on the phone looking for help rather than pay my nominal fee. Or, realistically, I guess I had not adequately communicated the value.

I went on to create a second business; this time a product-based business to switch things up and called it Yoshi-Bella Jewelry (after my dog). I dared not tell my veterinary colleagues about my extracurricular endeavours. I worried about what they would think! Once I let go of fear of judgement and shared my interests an interesting thing happened. Some of my colleagues told me that I had inspired them to reconnect with a passion they had as a child or teenager. Colleagues began reporting back to me about their lifted spirits in doing a creative outlet that they had forgotten in the mad rush to get to...where?

COMFORTABLE WITH **PARADOX,** I NOW LIVE FIRMLY ON THE FENCE BETWEEN ART AND SCIENCE, **BALANCING DATA WITH INTUITION, FACTS WITH FICTION, AND VEGETABLES WITH DESSERT.**

Personally, I've spent my life jumping off the plank. People always ask me how I seem to effortlessly just "do" things. It's been a lifetime of practicing taking creative leaps in my career and in my personal life. I even leapt when I decided to become a parent (don't tell my kids). I don't understand when people tell me, "they could never" backpack around the world solo for 14 months, rock climb, scuba dive, hike solo, perform stand-up, camp in the backcountry, meditate with sniper rifles in California, and get my kids to eat their vegetables. Ok, I might be exaggerating about one of those (*it's the vegetables*). They (and you) are no different from me, the difference is the jump. If you truly want to do something and you're scared, there are ways to hack that evolutionary drive to keep you safe. I'll share what I have learned from taking chances, leaping, and learning how to mitigate the risks and manage the fear. I don't consider myself a daredevil, and you don't need to be to expand your comfort zone. I hope that by sharing my process, you will find your own way to challenge comfort. I hope something will resonate with you, and that you can learn your own process to take small risks that improve your career and life. I tend to resist prescriptive, or "top 10 ways to" approaches, because I feel that we all have something important to share, and that there is no "right" way to live your life, despite what the gurus would have you believe. I'm writing this book because I know that accepting and encouraging your unique creative potential is the key to surviving and thriving this decade, and if one of the **D.A.N.C.E** habits helps you to get there, then it was all worthwhile. I hope this book will help you to feel more confident about when you should jump and when to stand still.

The only way to get better at something is to practice. How can you practice jumping off a plank? You can start with low-risk ways to stretch your comfort zone. Creativity is the diving board into the kiddie pool that you need to get started. Okay, bad analogy because that sounds like a really bad idea. I was trying to say that the kiddie pool is low risk, because it's small, and combine it with a diving board, because it still takes bold action to jump in. But you would probably break your neck. Revise!

CREATIVITY
IS THE TINY SLIDE INTO THE KIDDIE POOL INSTEAD OF THE HIGH DIVING BOARD.

There! I just gave you an example of being creative, leaping into the possibility of failure, and risking judgement.

1

Science Says,
"YOU ARE CREATIVE"

I was a creative genius in kindergarten. But, before you get too impressed, there's a 98% chance that you were also a creative genius in kindergarten. Sadly, there is also a 98% chance that you've lost it as an adult. You probably knew this already, but deep down it's a hard thing to admit. Adults will do a lot to rationalize their lack of creativity, telling themselves it is frivolous, unimportant, and ancillary to the important work and stress of "adulting."

My guess is that you picked up this book because you had an inkling your creativity has dissipated and you're hoping (but maybe reluctant?) to get it back.

Maybe you have read the studies that say creativity is the number one skill we need this decade and your interest is purely self-preserving. Or maybe you are feeling stuck, or stale, like a donkey, shackled to one of those flour wheels that grind wheat, walking around and around in the same circle until you die. Maybe you have reached the pinnacle of your career, by any measure of success, and still feel like "is this it?". It might feel like you just climbed a mountain only to find a view of the mall parking lot. You might wistfully recall the times you were happy, and truly joyful. These memories probably send you back to childhood when you could play and create without fear of judgement or assessment of an ROI (Return On Investment). Playing dress-up, writing your name in the snow with your pee, drawing your masterpiece on the bathroom wall in Sharpie marker, playing house and sending everyone to their rooms (wait, that's my adult life).

I'm not talking about feeling a bit stressed and tired—I'm talking about a more general sense of malaise, that ennui. The realization that your life has become boring and predictable. A pattern. This whole adulting thing has eaten you alive. Where'd you go?

Clueless and Creative in Kindergarten

In 1968, NASA commissioned Dr. George Land[2] to develop a creativity assessment. NASA wanted to identify which of their employees had creative potential. After the assessment was created, Dr. Land had a wild idea: How would kids score on the test? He administered the test to 1,600 kindergarteners—and guess what? A whopping 98% scored as "creative genius." My theory is that the other 2%

2 Find the link to Dr. Land's TED Talk under Ch. 1 at thereluctantcreative.com/resources

were too busy eating glue and pulling crayons out of their noses (which is also creative if you think about it). Dr. Land followed these kids through to 15 years old and noticed a gradual decrease in the creativity genius scores over time: down to 30% at 10 years old, then 12% at 15 years old. This same test was administered to 280,000 adults, with the whopping-ly underwhelming result of 2% of adults scoring as "creative genius."

The conclusion? We learn how not to be creative. Dr. Land proposes a solution; decrease the judgement, criticism, and censorship in education, which then also translates to the workplace. He tells us to find the five-year-old in each of us, by dreaming often and dreaming big. Five-year-olds don't worry about what others think of their dream to be an astronaut or a knee-deep exploration in a mud puddle.

If we were to ask the kindergarteners in Dr. Land's study to define creativity, they wouldn't understand.

TO A CHILD,
CREATIVITY IS LIFE.

Creativity is how they test and learn about the world; it's how they develop the knowledge and skills to survive. Ask most adults to define creativity, and they describe something artistic, something epic, something beyond their grasp, something for "others."

The definition of "creativity" is unclear, even to creativity researchers. One camp believes that creativity needs to be validated by peers in their domain, have novelty and usefulness. Does that then mean Vincent Van Gogh was not creative until after he died, since he didn't sell a single painting during his life?

Others, led by the work of Ruth Richards, believe that "everyday creativity" is accessible to all. Richards is an early pioneer of the idea of "everyday creativity." Her only two criteria are Originality and Meaningfulness. She explains that what you do is less important than how you do it. She also found some common factors to foster a creative environment. Groups should have an explorative mindset, collaborative, willing to take risks and be wrong, playful, no premature judgement, and willing to go with the flow of discovery. Other experts expand on the critical environment for creativity, with the need for freedom, autonomy, good role models and resources (including time), encouragement for originality, no criticism, and a focus on innovation despite failure. Free flowing ideas, shared knowledge and rewarding innovators adds more depth to the idea of collaboration.

Colour coded files, building a spreadsheet, or choosing what clothes to wear are examples of everyday creativity. Some researchers call everyday creativity "little c" creativity. "Big C" creativity is the type of art that you see in the Smithsonian, or an invention such as the iPhone. In this book, when I talk about creativity, I'm referring to everyday creativity, or "little c" creativity. This type of creativity is accessible to everyone. You are already doing it, but chances are, you simply don't recognize it as creativity because it seems so ordinary.

Dr. Marta Ockuly applied her background in business to the study of creativity. Dismissing the idea that creativity was defined by novelty and usefulness, she wrote her own definition based on 10 years of research. Dr. Ockuly's definition is "Creativity is the person centred process of imagined possibilities and taking embodied expressive action that makes your ideas real." This definition more accurately expresses what we know about creativity, our ubiquitous human gift, and has since been adopted by the World Creativity and Innovation Week Organization[3].

Creativity is an elemental human skill. Science has used technologies such as fMRI (functional magnetic resonance imaging) to look into our brains, leading to a deeper understanding of what happens as we create. From jazz improvisational musicians to Nobel Laureates, to Jessie from HR, the creative process is the same. Creativity is your human birthright. Just as you breathe without thinking and chew your food without much thought, creativity is pre-wired in your brain.

If Picasso painted while hooked up to an FMRI, we would see that his brain is doing the same things as the brain of Doug from accounting when he creates a new Pivot Table for his firm or when I sneak cooked broccoli into a

---

3   More information about World Creativity and Innovation Week can be found at this link under Chapter 1: thereluctantcreative.com/resources

strawberry banana smoothie. The great news? The benefits of creativity are universal, regardless of others' opinions. To reap the benefits of creativity, you can be really bad at it.

The good news is that you already possess creative potential, the bad news is that I can't just give it to you. Human creativity is as natural as breathing.

Let's consider breathing. Hopefully, you've nailed this one. But you can learn techniques to apply to your breathing for a desired outcome, like controlled box breathing for anxiety. Box breathing involves breathing in for a count of four, holding the breath for four counts, and exhaling for a count of four, holding the breath for four counts and then repeat. It's called box breathing because there are four steps, and it can be helpful to imagine a box while practising.

In the same way that box breathing can help anxiety, there are techniques that can help your creativity.

Let's reconsider those little creative geniuses of Dr. Land's research. What happens to our natural creativity? Do schools, in fact, drum it out of us? Turning us into assembly-line automatons to succumb to corporate bidding in a dissatisfying plod along the path of life to death? Sir Ken Robinson, a passionate creativity advocate, contended that it

is one of the great wrongs of our time that we squeeze the creativity out of children.

We do need to give ourselves some grace. Kindergarteners are creative when the answer does not require expertise, or when the situation calls for an unusual solution because kids have no idea how the world works. They're not really trying to be creative; they are just adorably clueless.

KIDS LEAD WITH A ZEN STYLE "BEGINNER MIND" BECAUSE THEY'RE LIFE'S TRUE BEGINNERS.

Curiosity helps learning, which seems obvious if you've ever gone on a road trip with a toddler. If we kept the cluelessness of a kindergartener as we aged, we would still be living in caves and using dial-up internet. Paradoxically, we would probably be in the same dark cave without *any* creativity.

As we grow, learn, and evolve, we make meaning from patterns. We create heuristics and shortcuts to get a sense of how the world works. We have survived because of this ability, to know instantly that the cat-like animal jumping through the grass is going to eat us, and not join us for dinner. If we had to invent a new way to light a fire every time, or a new method to hunt for food, we would not have survived as a species. However, giant leaps in evolution resulted from our ability to ask questions and to be curious. How did that fire start? How can I try to reproduce that? How would it help me? Why do burrs stick to my socks, and could that be helpful, someday turning into Velcro?

I agree with Sir Ken Robinson, that some blame lies with the educational system. In one of the most watched TED Talks of all time, he passionately advocates for a stronger role for creativity in education. As a mom of two teenagers, my heart hurts to imagine my sons sitting in class, passively digesting knowledge like a force-fed foie gras goose, only to regurgitate it later in a smelly mess. Where is the curiosity? Where is the love of learning? Where is the discomfort of ambiguity? Instead of an A or an F grade, how about an M for "Maybe" …?

Institutions are as easy to turn as a 1965 station wagon. I also know and appreciate that teachers are doing their best and that school is not the only culprit in this story. We are only doing what our species is designed to do: make sense of the world, find shortcuts for survival, and make another generation of our species. Corporations, families, media all promote this idea of finding your tribe, fitting in, towing the party line, supporting a deeply embedded evolutionary pull for survival — fit in or die. The instincts that scream at me to get off the stage during my stand-up comedy routine are the exact same instincts that helped humans survive. Exclusion from the tribe historically meant death from starvation, predation, or exposure. We, therefore, instinctively feel rejection as deeply as physical pain. Judgement of my own creative expression feels like the most hurtful rejection of all — the rejection of my genuine, true self that I trepidatiously share with the perilous world.

At this point, you might be thinking "Ok, so what if I am creative? Why bother if it hurts so much? What's it going to get me anyway?" If you are looking for the "how," feel free to skip ahead to Chapter Four — D. is for Daydream.

But first! A business case about creativity.

Creativity in Registry Lineups

Shannon Vander Meulen is a former teacher and entrepreneur who runs a registry business where people get driver and business licenses and more. When COVID-19 hit in March 2020, her registry business remained open, but she had to limit the capacity in her building. Customers had to wait outside prior to receiving service. Nobody wants to wait outside in Calgary, Alberta, Canada — we've been known to experience snow every month of the year. The bottleneck this limited capacity created had slowed down her transaction time, which impacted her business's bottom line, and irritated customers. One day, she sat on a bench near her business and watched the lethargic trickle into her store.

Shannon commits to spending time every day to think and **Daydream**. Like many business owners, the pandemic made her anxious and she was desperate for solutions. Instead of immersing herself in busy work, she slowed down and zoomed out for a big picture view. She got creative.

She observed the customers and traffic flow to her business. Customers hopped from foot to foot or shivered in their coats to stay warm, yet all customers stared at their phones. Shannon had a simple idea of using text notifications instead of a physical line to hold a spot. She started researching solutions and could not find anything that met her needs. Some registries were using a dedicated cell phone, but with 12 stations at her registry, she needed something more robust and automatic. Shannon partnered with a developer, where they built and tested their app Waitwell.ca[4] on the fly. Employee and customer feedback and continual testing helped to improve the accuracy of wait times, and a system to keep business flowing.

Once developed, the app helped staff see who was in line, what service they needed, and to alert their next customer. Shannon continued to observe and noticed that there was wasted time between when the customer received the text and when they met the employee, so she decided to implement a two-stage process, creating a COVID friendly "waiting room," to keep the foot traffic flowing.

---

4 Waitwell Line Management Software. Learn more at http://waitwell.ca/.

Shannon does not consider herself creative in an artistic sense, but it is creativity that fuels her passion for entrepreneurship. "I'm able to apply my skills and talents to solve problems in an open-ended way, rather than having someone direct me and say, 'I need you to find a solution to this problem and it needs to look just like this.' Instead, I'm able to determine what I think is the problem that needs to be solved and then explore all kinds of different options and try them out and put into play. I like to test different options and solutions to solve the problem in a way that works best for me."

Shannon uses all five of the effortless **D.A.N.C.E.** creative habits in her role as founder. Shannon **DAYDREAMS** when she imagines how it feels to be a customer, what they think and how they see the world, to try to see things from their point of view. Shannon practices engaging her tolerance of **AMBIGUITY** by asking open ended questions. Shannon loves the sales aspects of negotiating, not knowing how clients will respond, finding unique solutions for customers, and problem solving. To reach a new group of customers, Shannon practised the habit of **NOVELTY**. She identified some demographic and cultural groups that would benefit from her services, then intuitively used the creative problem-solving method of asking, "how might I reach these customers?" This approach took her down many rabbit holes, because there is not one clear path to reaching these customers. Shannon searched for unique approaches; Clubhouse audio, radio, other businesses and their strategies that were already reaching these customers and explored the unknown (to her) so she could get new ideas. **CURIOSITY** drove and continues to drive Shannon to relentlessly pursue research. At the nail salon, grocery story, or barbeque her insatiable curiosity drives her to collect new information all the time. "I just like getting information from people and sometimes I don't even have a purpose for asking. I just like to ask a lot of questions, and then just try to remember what they say, and I find that that often will pique an idea for me later."

Shannon **EDITS LATER** by chunking tasks. Structure provides a framework for her day, but with chunks of time to complete a general task, it gives her the flexibility to go off in a new direction and follow her intuition. As an entrepreneur, she has the flexibility to set her own priorities, and honour her natural rhythm, whether she chooses to write on one day, or find new markets on another. Although Shannon does not consider herself traditionally creative, she is drawn to writing and clearly engages her everyday creativity to constantly improve her successful business. We agreed in the interview that the touted five am entrepreneurial start time did not work for either of us. Shannon gets her best ideas when she is rested, when she has space and time to think, without task laden busy work. Her best epiphanies come when she is walking her dog, usually alone, but surrounded by other dog parents. Shannon's awareness of her creative amplifiers and obstacles helps her to structure her schedule and business to capitalize on things that others might be missing. "You need to focus on working ON the business, not IN the business," she suggests.

Keeping Shannon — and the other plank jumping moms — in mind, let's now dig into why fear of judgement holds us back, and how engaging with our everyday creativity will help us get over ourselves as being "not creative." Spoiler alert, it's got nothing to do with finger painting or basket weaving, unless that's what you're drawn to.

Haha, get it? Drawn to?

Fear of Judgement: Our Creative Frenemies

Judgement. The one thing that stops so many of us from realizing our own unique everyday creative gifts. Also, the one thing that stops us from clicking the link in that text from the tax office. Judgement is not all bad, but when it comes to creativity there are two main barriers:

1. Our inner critic. This is the inner voice that is so critical of you that it sometimes can unconsciously stop you from even expressing yourself at all. Sometimes, we confuse this voice with our own. I personally call my inner critic "Todd" so I know it's not my voice. This lets me **D.A.N.C.E.** in everyday creativity. Todd comes back again in other chapters, so keep an eye out for his critical voice.

2. Our fear of criticism and judgement from others.

Turn a frown upside down!

How can you transform these inner criticisms to positive affirmations? Add or remove some words, be creative!

YOU'RE STUPID.   Why would you do that?

That doesn't make any sense.

Are you for real?

You don't fit in.

 YOU DON'T MATTER, I CANNOT RELATE TO YOU.

I don't want to be around you anymore.

Isn't this really what's holding us back from expressing our creativity? Most of us haven't shared our inner creative selves to the world since kindergarten. Remember, when we were all creative geniuses? Before we learned that "others" have an opinion on how we interact with the world? Maybe you remember that first moment that you shared a masterpiece with a well-meaning, truth telling adult who felt the need to tell you that your doughnuts in your painting were not "doughnutty" enough. Maybe you remember your dismay as you plonked your science project on the chipped gymnasium table and looked around at the incredible feats made by the other students. Maybe you were the kid with the amazing science project and felt deflated because you knew it wasn't your work. Your parents made it for you when they thought yours wasn't good enough, that it would be too embarrassing (for you or for them?). At some point you realized that your creativity just didn't add up to much. Ouch.

I remember one of my early brushes with rejection and failure. I wanted to do something *different* for my grade two talent show at school. I thought I would try ventriloquism because why not?! It seemed pretty cool. I waited my turn after the kid who had been taking piano since she was three, or the eloquent poetry reader. I could have played the piano; I was good enough. I could have sung a song, which would have been…not too sweet. I could have even touched my nose with my tongue (true story). But ventriloquism was sweetly unusual. I had practiced, lots, but ventriloquism is not an easy thing to pick up in a week or two. As a child, I didn't realize how hard it was and saw my efforts from the vantage point of my naïve young optimistic mind. I was always one of those kids. Sure, I had friends, but I spoke too loudly, made too much of a mess of my desk and handwriting, I interrupted too much and laughed too loud (thanks a lot, ADHD and 1980's era misogyny). I started my rehearsed set with a smile and my Cabbage Patch doll, Pierrette, on my lap. I looked out at my classmates and my teacher's faces and the realization of my grave error swept through me like a tsunami. I could see it reflected back at me. The judgement, the scorn, the "otherness" repelled me like a negative battery charge. At least, that's how I felt. Maybe they were stunned into silence by the magnificence of my amateur ventriloquism talent. But I interpreted the silence as scorn, leaving me feeling humiliated. This pain of humiliation was as real and crippling as if I had been punched in the stomach.

After that experience, it might seem strange that I would want to try stand-up comedy, the penultimate test of facing judgement of others, standing alone on a stage. Perhaps I have an inner performer that will not be denied? Most people are terrified of the thought of performing stand-up comedy. There's a reason they call it "dying" or "bombing" on stage. Veteran comics say that all stand-up comics bomb, or fail onstage, at some point. So, I guess I should have expected it in the earliest part of my stand-up comedy adventure. My not-so-hero's perilous journey began in a stand-up class, in the living room of a duplex in a trendy Calgary neighbourhood, the office for a local comedy festival. I graduated to uproarious applause from my husband, two friends, and fellow classmates. I was ready for my HBO TV special. Instead, I agreed to host a fundraising comedy event for a local charity. My job as host and MC was to warm up the audience, do some comedy, introduce the Executive Director, and tell people when to eat (the most important part). I had prepared ahead of time by interviewing the executive director to get inside dirt on the organization's key players. I rehearsed and proudly timed my set to the second. I researched how to be a great host. I knew it would be great, even without Pierrette at my side.

I started with personalized jokes, confidently using audience work to warm up the crowd, call out organization celebrities, and keep the flow moving. So far, so good. People were laughing! I was having a great time. This was fun, I felt good. Time to call dinner! Confident, I stepped on stage to give the audience a five-minute warning. I chatted with the headline and other feature comics. I felt like a true performer, accepted as one of their guild. I strode on stage, pulled the microphone from its stand, and started my set. This was it, the easy part, my rehearsed set, my "good material."

My first joke landed on deaf ears. There were five people in the front row politely listening to my set, and the rest of the room might as well have been a pack of cats in a field of catnip. One table, with their backs to me, noisily hijacked a passing audience member to take their photo. Another lady in the centre of the room stood up and called to her friend Rosie; "Over here, Rosie, we're sitting here!" My confidence dissolved into dejection. Panicked, I did what most people do in uncertainty, I went to a status quo solution. Like a tourist in a foreign country, I delivered my jokes louder, the panic welling up in my stomach. I glanced at the waiting comics. I knew I was letting them down. As the host, it was my job to warm up the audience, get them engaged and laughing, and start the evening off right.

I finished the set, introduced the feature comic, and ran off stage as quickly as I could. I had bombed. Hard. The feature comic struggled for most of his set to warm up the audience, and it was my fault.

I had to stay until the end of the show because I was the MC. I didn't want to thank the audience. In that moment though, I hated the audience. While I knew it was my fault, I petulantly — and silently — whined at their lack of consideration. But I knew I had bombed. I didn't do my job and I had been in over my head. I walked to the end of the plank and jumped. It was painful to watch the video footage of my set. The audience view showed a group of people completely uninterested in my performance. I shared the most vulnerable part of myself, my creativity, and I was rejected. Rejection that felt like physical pain. Rejection of creative work, which is so personal, cuts especially deeply. This pain is what holds us back from expressing our creativity — our authentic, unique voice with the world.

The only way to get better at anything, including judgement and failure, is to do it. If you, like me, are mid-career, you are likely used to being good at your job. You've lost your kindergartener's clueless comfort with failure and trying new things. Granted, a five-year-old belting out Adele while dressed in a pixie outfit wearing bunny slippers might be a bit more acceptable than a middle-aged HR executive. Or is it? I guess that depends on your goal. If your goal is to sit in your box waiting to die, then the pixie outfit isn't for you. But, if you want to look back and feel confident that you lived a regret-proof life, took some chances to be uncomfortable, knowing that failure is the price to pay? Priceless.

The simple truth is that nobody cares that much about what you do anyway. The physical pain you feel from rejection that lasts for days, is an outdated survival mechanism. Dude from the front row has already forgotten my set as he walked out of the club door. Sometimes the people who seem to care about what you do are only critical because they are terrified to share their own creativity, and it threatens the order of their universe to see someone else fearlessly sharing their own. Crabs in a bucket will pull down the other crabs to prevent their escape. It's all a matter of perspective and that's what we're exploring. Now, knowing that you are creative, and why you resist sharing it with the world, let's find out why it matters. After all, as we'll soon learn, creativity can help you take chances. After all, experts agree that creativity is the number one skill that you needed yesterday.

LUCKILY,
IT'S NOT TOO LATE.
CREATIVITY
IS LIKE POOP.
YOU'RE FULL OF IT.
LET'S FIND THAT
CREATIVITY EX-LAX TO
GET YOUR CREATIVITY
FLOWING.

2

Benefits of D.A.N.C.E.(ing) with Everyday Creativity

rowing up my creative pursuits were tolerated. I was allowed to explore creativity so long as I studied hard, and school still came first. Exercising individual creative freedom was seen as fun, frivolous, and ancillary to the main goal of life, to get a "good" job, memorize all the facts, and contribute to society. Sound familiar?

Since the Industrial Revolution began, there has been shift away from everyday creativity. We have prioritised productivity, providing for your family, getting a promotion, gaining respect from neighbours, even memorizing the Kreb's cycle (yes, I'm still sore about it). Where is the time or room for individual expression? I think that most people realize that creative hobbies can be interesting or fun, like a chocolate indulgence after dinner.

What many people don't realize is that exercising creativity has immense personal and professional benefits. This ROI is hard to quantify because it doesn't feel like work.

When you start to **D.A.N.C.E.** with the five key habits to increase your creativity today, you will start to see the benefits documented by science. The first thing you will notice is a better mood, especially the next day. Then, you might see that you are more satisfied at work and feel more effective as you learn to speak out more at meetings and share your opinions, leading to better performance reviews. You will start to risk-assess and tell your inner critic to find something else to do, while you share your creative ideas. This newfound pep in your step at work will be noticed by your team, and you will start getting bigger and better roles, solving harder problems, and possibly earn a promotion. When you negotiate your next raise, you might get more money, since creators report a higher salary than non-creators.

Every time you take a chance to speak up in a meeting, try something new in the kitchen, or wear a new style of clothes, you build resilience to face uncertainty, obstacles, and fear of judgement. Your "just do it[5]" muscle will get stronger and stronger, and with it, the respect from others as you march to the rhythm of your own drum.

---

5 Thank you, Nike, for this superb tagline!

"SO WHAT IF I'M CREATIVE? WHY DOES THIS MATTER TO ME?"

Creative Forecast for Innovation

Creativity matters even if you only want a good job or a successful business. Sure, it is one of those amorphous "soft skills," one might even call a bandwagon. Here's the thing, LinkedIn proclaimed, "Creativity as the number one skill in 2020." In an older study of CEOs from 2009, IBM concluded that creativity was the most important leadership skill. Dell predicted in 2017 that 85% of the jobs in 2030 don't even exist yet. Bloomberg echoed that Creative Problem Solving one of the most desired but hardest to find skill sets in 2016. McKinsey determined that the top missing skills areas are problem solving, critical thinking, innovation, and creativity. The World Economic Forum predicts that by 2025, 85 million jobs will have been displaced by AI and robots, and 97 million new jobs will be created, with what top required skill? Analytical thinking and innovation. You can't shake a stick at a stockholder meeting without hitting a company with innovation as a core value. The importance of innovation is recognized by

92% of companies and is a prerequisite to adapt to the current pace of change. Yet, well before we find innovation, there must be creativity at the individual and team level.

Innovation Starts With the Letter I

I is for the individual who allows their creativity to play, who has the expertise to develop feasible ideas, and the confidence to share it with others so that the idea can be shaped into a true innovation. Innovation starts with the individual team members. Innovation strategy, mission statements, and declarations of support for innovation are wasted without a focus on the individual in the company. Anit Somech and Anat Drach-Zahavy investigated conditions that influence innovation implementation. The first key drivers included the average creative score of individuals within a team, meaning that teams made up of creative individuals are more creative (uh, duh!). Additionally, highly creative teams were made up of a heterogeneous mix of different organizational roles, knowledge, and skills. The main factor allowing creative ideas to become innovations was a culture of innovation within the organization, with psychological safety for team members to express creative ideas.

The great thing about creativity is the opportunity to differentiate yourself and your organization. Most of the 92% of companies who want innovation are getting it wrong, since only 18% of employees feel like they can take risks at work to be creative. Talk about low hanging fruit. This fruit will ripen in a climate that promotes creative expression, psychological safety, and collaboration, or rot in a climate of micromanagement, strict rules, and a culture of achievement over experimentation.

Exercising your creativity can also help you improve your life at home. May I offer you some mood benefits or some confidence in uncertainty, perhaps?

If you like proof, hold onto your Bonferroni[6] (nerdy stats joke!) because this chapter is full of it. Proof, not poop. Remember — you are the one who is full of poop. And creativity, of course.

Corporate Creativity

Companies know they need creativity. Consultants know that companies need creative employees, but nobody wants to call it out. Corporations use words like "innovation" and "think differently" to avoid the kumbaya-macrame vibe of the word "creativity." Companies overwhelmingly recognize the importance of innovation, yet creativity can still conjure images of glue-eating preschoolers, elderly patients in care facilities, or paint splattered artists. In an unofficial poll of my clients, most associate creativity with painting or other visual arts. A perilously unscientific result, I must admit.

Creativity in business is still a pariah. Most companies don't want a granola eating hippie covered in paint and smelling of patchouli in their board room. Yet, leaders know

---

6   Bonferroni correction is a conservative test that, although protects from Type I Error, is vulnerable to Type II errors (failing to reject the null hypothesis when you should in fact reject the null hypothesis). For more, and for a sure cure for insomnia, find the link under Ch. 2 at thereluctantcreative.com/resources

that innovation is important. There is also an academic, possibly begrudging admission that creative problem solving and critical thinking are instrumental to become leaders in their market.

If only creativity could be, well, less creative. Let's explore some tangible ways to increase creativity and how they lead to business results.

ENTER — DIVERSITY.

Innovation arises from a team with diversity and unique perspectives, within a psychologically safe environment. An innovative team welcomes diversity, thrives with flexibility and support, and is possibly even celebrated for failing. However, simply having a culturally diverse team is not enough to prompt significant creativity. Team members must differ in deep level attributes like cultural values and worldviews to reap a benefit of team diversity on creativity. Diversity can help to buffer against groupthink. In the book, *In Defence of Troublemakers,* Charlan Nemeth describes the benefit of thoughtful and genuine dissent to bolster better decisions and problem solving.

Team members must tap into their own individual well of creativity, including having the awareness of which environments, mindsets and conditions are required for their creative success. Critically, an employee will only explore their creative potential in a culture that supports experimentation, failure, and cross-functional collaboration.

Natasha Purnell, Chief Culture Officer at Park Insurance, uses her personal creativity to engage employees and achieve a 94% employee satisfaction score[7]. She attributes her success to leaning into her creativity, taking chances, and risking failure. One of her early ideas was a plank challenge to support wellness initiatives. Over 12 weeks, participants built up to a two-minute plank. The success gave her confidence to lean into her creativity. Natasha had to round up the team, who resisted at first, but once they started seeing results, she noticed an increase in trust between each other and in her ability to lead through creativity. Natasha's ideas are not necessarily new ideas, but she curates and adapts them to her organization and goals. She works hard to foster a creative environment that supports change and adaptation, with the necessary safety for employees in the event of failure, resulting in a culture of innovation and safety.

In a Gallup study of more than 16,500 employees, they found three necessary factors to foster employee creativity, all of which Natasha employed in her creativity engagement:

1. An expectation to be creative at work. E.g., Natasha rounding up her team for their creative challenge.

2. Allotted time to be creative. E.g., Setting a specific time to do their plank exercise at work.

3. Freedom to take the risks necessary to be creative. E.g., Natasha willingly models how to take risks and shows that there is safety if the ideas fail.

---

7 Find the interview with Natasha under Ch. 2 at thereluctantcreative.com/resources

Workplaces that support creativity, like at Park Insurance, have higher levels of personal, team and organizational performance. Employees who feel supported to be creative feel like they are doing their best work and half as likely to say they're looking for another job.

Corporate creativity impacts beyond employee satisfaction. McKinsey & Company link creativity to a business' value, finding a correlation between above average financial performance and a creativity score. Creativity among teams has also been shown to increase team cohesion, which has been shown to be a key driver of business success.

Shhh...Call It "Think Differently"

Unfortunately, there is no clear consensus among creativity researchers on the definition of creativity. So, how do we know what companies really want when they say they want "creativity?" Apparently, it depends on who you ask.

Dr. Jennifer Mueller explains in her book, *Creative Change*, that creativity is in the eye of the beholder. Decision makers define creativity in terms of feasibility, profitability, and ease of implementation. Employees define creativity in terms like risk, unproven, and unique. Decision makers are prone to a creativity bias, whereby they avoid new ideas in favour of tried-and-true strategies. With your butt on the line, facing uncertainty, you'll choose status quo solutions, perhaps unconsciously. How many times have you talked to coworkers who bemoan the lack of originality in leadership? You may notice that as some coworkers rise in the corporate ranks, they tend to become more risk averse, more rigid, and less open to new ideas. Our default position, even if we are not a decision maker, is to be suspicious of creativity. Ironically, since we are comfortable with bosses who have as much originality as a chicken nugget, we react in fear and alarm when our boss starts challenging norms. Originality triggers a threat response, even if it is a nicer and more effective version than the original. The threat of a radical new approach intensifies when risk is assessed by the person who will ultimately be responsible for failure. Many other factors influence how ideas are received, including gender, previous knowledge and experience, perception of creativity, and how "out-of-this-world" the idea is.

Close your eyes (ok, well, squint, so you can still read). Imagine a ballet dancer who presents ways to leverage your third quarter results to maximize tax advantages to increase stockholder returns. A threat response sweeps through your brain because the idea theme (finance) does not match the source (ballet dancer). The conflicting condition, known as cognitive dissonance, results from the inconsistency between your beliefs and what is presented in front of you. We hate cognitive dissonance, so we cleverly make it go away.

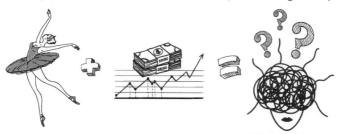

When we register this incongruence, we feel uncertain. The situation does not fit what we expect. We might tell ourselves that the idea would have merit if it was just a little more "original." Or that it would be so creative if it was not quite so linear. As Jamie Holmes explains in *Nonsense*, the threat response can trigger anxiety, even if it is a positive experience. Remember that boss who always yelled at you? Now, imagine they surprise you with a free lunch, then kindly suggest you complete the overdue report, when you have time. Threat response ignited! I would be thinking "I guess I'm getting fired today!" or "What alien possessed my boss?" When faced with ambiguity, we feel uncertain, sometimes to the point of skepticism. Our senses are on high alert, seeking more data.

IS THERE A THREAT? DOES IT LOOK, FEEL, SOUND, SMELL **SAFE?**

When companies say they need creativity, they don't fully recognize what creativity looks, feels, or smells like. So, who knows what they really want? They can't even tell you what they want. Look, the Spice Girls can't even tell you what they want, what they really really want.

Do you have an unconscious bias against creativity? Well, wait...an unconscious bias means you don't know you have it by definition, so…are you sure? If you have a very strong immediate reaction to something — positive or negative — it's a clue to self-check in for any bias.

Your Mood and Creativity

New research presented by Adam Grant in his 2021 TED Talk showed that during the pandemic, the biggest predictor of happiness was flow[8]. Flow, a condition where time seems to stand still. Flow, where you don't notice anything else because you are so immersed in the experience. So many people find flow when they are engaging their creativity.

WHO WANTS TO BE UN-HAPPY?

Everyday "little c" creativity, like making and then eating a healthy meal, makes you feel better the next day. Many studies have found a strong link between creativity and happiness, but research found that creativity has a direct effect on increasing positive affect (like happiness) the following day. Then, guess what! You're in such a great mood, that you are more inclined to be creative. A beautifully delicious chocolate chicken and the Easter Cream egg!

During COVID, researchers Hansika Kapoor and James Kaufman elaborate on the ways that creativity have helped people find meaning during the pandemic. Citing the benefits of journaling, enjoying works of art, immersion

---

8 Watch Adam Grant's full Ted Talk under Ch. 2 at thereluctantcreative.com/resources

into a creative "flow" state as beneficial ways to find coherence, to improve wellbeing during the pandemic, Kapoor describes four types of "C" creativity seen during COVID. From leaders creating new ways to get PPE to those who needed them, to YouTubers making people laugh (my kids, anyway — I still don't know what's so funny about it) to Bollywood actors helping itinerant workers get home from Mumbai, creativity has burgeoned in response to the constraints of a global pandemic.

In another study from Argentina, participants said they engaged various creative activities during quarantine, to search for joy, a means to cope, or sharing with others. The creative activities generated positive emotions and helped them cope with the negative emotions in response to the pandemic.

What did you do during the pandemic that helped to lift your mood? Did you jump on the bread making bandwagon, or grow some plants, or even create an office space in your home that made things a bit more bearable? The pandemic made us tap into our everyday creativity even if we didn't know we were doing so.

Many other studies have documented the correlation between creativity and positive states. Creative activity has been shown to increase well-being in several groups including nurses, older students, family caregivers of cancer patients, and a wider diversity of individuals in the US. University students who expressed creativity had significantly higher emotional, psychological, and social well-being. When a group of knitters responded to a survey, a significant effect was found between frequency of knitting and on feeling calm and happy, as well as cognitive function. Knitting in a group significantly improved perceived happiness and social connection.

I could go on and on...but the point is that creativity directly correlates to mood and our overall wellbeing.

But WHY does creativity make you happier? New research suggests that we love creativity because we love problem solving. Making a meal, creating a customer journey map, choosing a screensaver, taking a photo of the sunset all involve problem-solving. Creators are better problem solvers, and this makes us happy. Simple?

One of my favourite things about the happy boost from creativity, is that you don't even have to be good at your creative outlet of choice to get the creative benefits. Take the chance on your creativity unless, of course, you have already maxed out your happiness and wellbeing. *I thought so.* My children do not share my learned optimism of the well-being benefits of listening to my singing, however.

Working 9 to 5 in 2025

Imagine the graduating high school class of 2025. In that broad sea of optimistic faces, 85% of them will find a job that has not yet been invented. Massive changes in workforce structure are happening at an incredible pace. I see it at my grocery store, when I'm greeted by the newly minted team in charge of sanitizing hands, carts, and checking for masks. New jobs since the pandemic include contact tracing experts, PPE experts and industries, remote working tech development and COVID related support for businesses, infrastructure, and education.

Let's break out the DeLorean from Back to the Future and head to 2025. The World Economic Fund predicts that 85 million jobs will have been displaced by robots, with 97 million new roles to take their place. How do you prepare yourself for a future that you cannot predict? "What do you want to do when you grow up" seems like a waste of time, without a crystal ball. If you're reading this book in 2025... were they right?

Maybe advancement and promotion are not on your agenda. Maybe you just want to feel more fulfilled with the job you have, or to feel like what you do matters. People who consider themselves creative or engage their creativity "fairly often" have higher job satisfaction. Additionally, they tend to score up to 30% better on performance ratings.

Logically, this makes sense. If every day creative activities increase your mood the following day, wouldn't that make going to work a lot more pleasant?

If you want to go through life miserable (don't call me, I'll call you), money might compel you to reconsider your drive to create. Creative employees were paid 13% more. If you could take a skill you already have, make some room for it to thrive, and get more money, job satisfaction and profitability, wouldn't you do it? This is really the best kept secret to your success this decade. But it's not just about getting the "best" job anymore, due to the massive changes coming to the workforce.

No More Working on the Railroad
All the Live Long Day

The next decade is going to shake things up, with over four million Canadians, and 375 million people worldwide (14% of the workforce) needing to retrain or completely change careers to stay in the workforce. RBC predicts that up to 50% of jobs will require significant reskilling. The "gig" economy is here, with workers expected to rapidly pivot, acquire new skills, and flex their skills to the needs of the moment. A 2020 Monster.ca poll found that 92% of job seekers think that now is a good time to look into entering the gig workforce. NASA and other highly innovative organizations are already on board with gig workers, open talent and innovation. Steve Rader started at NASA as a flight engineer, and helped launch the International Space Station, among other incredible achievements. Steve is the Program Manager of the NASA Tournament Lab and the Centre of Excellence for Collaborative Innovation. Open innovation "competitions" help to source ideas globally from a wide variety of industries. Winners get a cash prize, and sometimes there are multiple winning ideas. Steve also uses open talent techniques to find unique specialists in their domain to help solve a very specific problem, instead of expecting NASA scientists to have all the answers. The result is a highly collaborative, integrated, and innovative environment. One of the challenges for companies, Steve explains, is to be able to balance the creative portion of innovation with the implementation and action requirements. The creative portion only accounts for about one percent of the entire project, with the bulk spent on logistics, supply chain, and implementation. The environment required for innovation to thrive is counter to an environment for productivity and action, so it can be a challenge to do both well. Without a proper focus on innovation, with time and effective techniques to create and brainstorm, you get a sub-optimal result, which might be an incremental improvement but not disruptive. Many companies are following NASA's lead and using open talent and open innovation to inject fresh ideas and important expertise at strategic points on their innovation journey.[9]

If you feel competent today, and like it that way, a reckoning is coming. To stay relevant in the workforce, you will have to deliberately seek the discomfort of being bad at something new. There is no longer a choice. You can run, but you can't hide, from the expectation of new skills acquisition to stay employed in a perpetual series of gig contracts.

Creative Resilience and Failure for Fun

Resilience: The quality or fact of being able to recover quickly or easily from, or resist being affected by, a misfortune, shock, illness, etc.; robustness; adaptability.

One great way to build resilience is to deliberately suck at something new. If you have a few years of work under your belt, you have likely not sucked at something professionally for a while. You have probably developed some core skills, learned some new things on the way, but overall feel competent with the skills in your tool belt.

When you stand in front of a blank easel, stare at an empty Excel spreadsheet, or stand in front of the fridge searching for ingredients, you are facing uncertainty. Any creative practice is like boot camp to build strength in the perilous land of ambiguity. To step into a creative practice takes vulnerability to face the unknown, which means to face the possibility of failure. It starts with curiosity and vulnerability. If you never face failure and uncertainty, how can you rebound from it? I'm not suggesting you deliberately face failure in a shareholder meeting or at the top of a double black ski run. The consequences are scary and potentially harmful. But what if you could get a bit better at facing failure and uncertainty when it didn't really matter? You can learn to hack your outdated survival mechanism that makes you feel rejection the same way as physical pain and discover that this rule is obsolete. Small creative failures along the way.

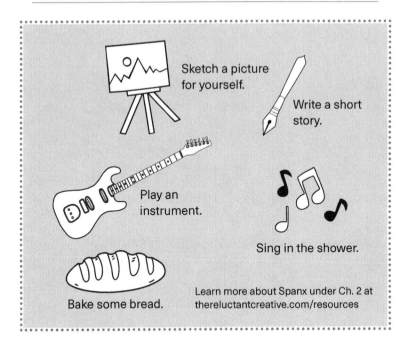

Sketch a picture for yourself.

Write a short story.

Play an instrument.

Sing in the shower.

Bake some bread.

Learn more about Spanx under Ch. 2 at thereluctantcreative.com/resources

Failing isn't fun...yet we fail spectacularly well when we do something for the first time. From there, we find our comfort zone and settle in for the long haul. I don't know about you, but I would rather not "settle in" to the one life I have to live. But what do we usually regret? We regret times we found comfort instead of uncertainty. We regret avoiding that uncomfortable conversation and eventually losing the chance to speak. We regret squishing ourselves in the box that others use to define who we are, like a metaphysical (or metaphorical) full body Spanx[10]. There is a part of us that wants to break out and be different, but it doesn't fit the narrative of who we are "supposed" to be. We stay safe

---

10 Although, I do appreciate a good pair of Spanx thanks to founder Sara Blakely. Learn more about Spanx under Ch. 2 at thereluctantcreative.com/resources

by staying small, quiet, and avoiding what we perceive to be "failure," to stay in the tribe like everyone else. Bronnie Ware, an Australian nurse working with the terminally ill, described the poignant conversations she had with dying patients. Dying patients didn't regret the chances they took, but the chances they didn't take. The number one regret was **"I wish I'd had the courage to live a life true to myself, not the life others expected of me."** Most people had not honoured even a half of their dreams, due to the choices they had made.

Everyday creativity helps you to practice failure while also revealing that failure is not the end of anything, it is just the beginning. With respect to my stand-up comedy "career," I enjoy doing it, and I get laughs, but I'm not ready to commit to the 20,000 hours it supposedly might take to possibly, maybe, fingers-crossed, get a break and "make it." I perform for myself, and if I'm honest, I also perform for others, but not in the way you might think. Not to make them laugh or have a good night out. I tell jokes to the person in the audience who sees a middle-aged mom and veterinarian standing up and telling jokes about her life, and thinks, *Wow, if she can do that, maybe I can do that thing I've been scared of, too.*

LAUGHS ARE GOOD, THOUGH. I'LL THROW MY EGO A BONE.

Freedom to Fail

In most "little c" creative endeavours, your failure only really matters to you. The goal is to get past your inner critic. You might know someone who doesn't seem to care about making a mistake or about saying something "dumb." These brazen performers have practised stepping off the plank of safety, over and over and over. Practice helps you realize that the consequences aren't as bad as you imagined (the perilous paradox of your creative imagination limiting your creativity). This is why I share my videos of learning the guitar, my failed culinary, and artistic...experiments. There is freedom for me in simply Not. Giving. A. Flying. Fox about how others will perceive my "failure." I can gleefully (and honestly, sometimes a bit smugly — hey, I'm human too!) share my failures and know that it does not reflect upon my self-worth, nor my competence in other domains. Why? It's practice. The more I share my "failures" with the world, the less I care about how others think about my failures. How meta.

When I started sharing some of my creative endeavours, like building Yoshi-Bella, my online jewelry company, I noticed a surge of coworkers who told me about their rediscovered creativity. My unapologetic pursuit of my inner creativity gave others permission to seek their own.

Are You Feeling Lucky?

Audience members, colleagues, and friends tell me that they are inspired by my willingness to step into uncertainty and failure. They often say things like "I could never do that," "I think it's amazing that you do stand-up," or, my kids favourite, "Stop singing. Stop!" Yet, it's the fear of judgement which holds people back from stepping out and unapologetically owning their experiments, their failures, and their creativity.

At the end of Chapter One, we began to explore our inner critic (remember Todd?) and fear of other's criticism. It's time for our deep dive into these creative (fr)enemies in detail!

 Creativity Enemy #1. Internal Judgement.

Remember — our inner critic, our internal judgment, is the inner mean critic who sometimes even unconsciously stops you from expressing yourself. This inner critic might even say things that make a lot of sense, like "you're too tired," or "do it tomorrow," or "you don't really want to do that, do you?" Steven Pressfield explains the origins of what he calls "The Resistance" in his book, the *War of Art*. The resistance, he says, always expresses itself in a reasonable argument, using rationality to derail your advance to creative expression. Pressfield has this ability to see through the masks and excuses we use to justify our creative cowardice. He cuts succinctly and precisely to the core of what holds us back from expressing creativity. Reading Pressfield's book makes me feel both understood and exposed at the same time. Like I have been photographed with my mouth full of crumbs and my hand in the cookie jar, but by a therapist who explains the reasons why I can't help myself.

 Creativity Enemy #2. External Judgement, Fear of Criticism. How do artists who publicly share their work get past this fear and do it anyway? Are they wired differently, or made of Teflon? Brittany Lyseng is a rising star in the Canadian comedy scene. She transitioned from elevator mechanic to full time comedian a few years ago. In our interview, Brittany shared that her fear of judgement and failure never goes away. One of the things that helps her overcome this fear, is to look at the failure as a learning experience, and by redirecting her focus to the audience experience, instead of worrying about whether she will be "good." Brittany believes that creativity is showing people what's in your heart and putting that passion into your life and making things. An olive branch from you to somebody else to show them what you're thinking, like when Brittany's mom makes a meal, or her dad creates something from wood.[11]

What can we do when the judgy voices speak up? *Objective Risk Mitigation.*

I have identified my own personal pattern whenever I face a challenge, like this summer when I agreed to a four-day backpacking trip in bear country.

---

11 Interview with Brittany can be found under Ch. 2 at thereluctantcreative.com/resources

1. Enthusiastically agree to the trip. Wait, where are we going?

2. Have second thoughts about whether I will enjoy it, will it be too hard, can I spare the time away, and how much I hate sleeping in a tent.

3. Ask "what is the worst that can happen?" Well, I could get attacked by a bear or die of exposure. But probably not — I've been on these trips before, and I know how to prepare. Lots of people hike in the backcountry and most turn out fine.

4. Almost cancel. I have that thing. My toe hurts. I need to clean my toilet.

5. Wish I could give up but see this predictable pattern appearing. Oh, this is just the part where I get nervous about the uncertainty and try to find comfort by cancelling.

6. Wonder what all the fuss was about in the first place. Get some sleepless nights, eat bad food, have a close call with a bear who didn't care about us at all, and see the most majestic sights that can only be accessed by hiking. Including a Bald Eagle missing a lunch of duckling by a few millimetres and endangered caribou grazing in the distance.

These steps repeat when I exercise my creativity. Knowing the pattern, and seeing the resistance as part of the process, is a critical piece of self-awareness. If you can see it, you can fight it.

I see you. You can't fool me.

Whether it's a hard hike, a performance, speaking up at a meeting, or making that difficult phone call, keep your enemies to excellence close and call them out when you see them coming. Acknowledge and ignore.

One of my favourite techniques is to name your inner naysayer. You can use the name I've given mine — Todd — or choose your own naysayer name.

"Hey Todd, thanks for coming out. I know you want to sit on the couch and eat Cheetos, but I want to haul my butt up a mountain today. Then we can eat Cheetos."

I forget much of what I do, thanks to ADHD (Think, forget. Think, forget). I call myself a monitor with no hard drive. This is problematic in many areas of my life, but not in the part that helps me expand my comfort zone. Since I forget bad (and good) feedback, and many details about the things in my life, they can't hold me back. Don't get me wrong, there are plenty of things that get stuck in my over-thinking infinity loop. Yet, I will quickly and easily contact someone that inspires me, regardless of fame or notoriety. I assume that if they are too busy to answer, then I won't get an answer. And if they are not too busy to answer, they might really appreciate my message. If they are too busy to answer, then they are certainly too busy to worry about my email.

It's in this willingness to be uncomfortable that an opportunity smacked me in the face right at the midpoint of my writing journey for this very book.
I'm a big fan of bestselling author Daniel Pink's work. His writing is pleasingly funny, humble, yet evidence based (remember — I love and need the data). He balances the rigor of research with interesting stories and writing to make learning fun. *A Whole New Mind* helped launch me on my current passion for sharing the importance of creativity. I believe every service provider, including veterinarians, should read *To Sell is Human. Drive,* I believe, is the best book on motivation I've read thus far. Clearly, I'm a huge fan, so when he sent out a call in his newsletter and on LinkedIn to find people with a "No Regrets" tattoo to interview for his next book, I felt called to respond to the request…despite not having one of these tattoos myself.

I wasn't expecting a response back. Todd woke up from his nap to share his thoughts as I composed my email to this author I respect and admire.

"He's too busy."

"He'll think I'm stupid for expecting that he would read my email."

"He probably doesn't even read his own emails."

"I'm sure he already found someone with a No Regrets tattoo."

"What if he will think I'm dreaming if I think I can write a book?"

"What if he is offended by my insolent request and rants publicly about my arrogance?"

"What if he reads my email?"

"What if I can help him with his book?"

"What if he is a really nice guy and appreciates the connection?"

"What if he likes my book?"

"What's the worst that can happen?"

Yet, much to my pleasant surprise, Daniel Pink himself responded! The thing to highlight here is that I took a risk. Then I took action. This all resulted in Mr. Pink agreeing to read this book and write a lovely jacket quote you see on the cover!

Of course…it may not always work out. There was that one time I tried to make a collect call to George Michael (Wham!) in London, from the Stone Road Mall in Guelph, Ontario. Yet, I'm still here, there is no celebrity-contacting-police that put me in jail or sent me a fine for reaching out respectfully to people who I admire. I detached my actions from the narrative around the outcome. By keeping our integrity and consideration of others as our True North, we allow ourselves to play in the waves more easily.

When faced with creative resistance, learn to identify the steps in your own process, such as the one I highlighted on page 57. You can do this if you practice stepping into the uncertainty of creativity often enough. Practice might not make perfect, but it certainly helps. Developing your self awareness around your own resistance allows you to focus on risk evaluation, detach from the judgement of others and from the outcome of personal expression.

I am genuinely astounded by the incredible benefits of exercising our own unique style of human creativity. Ongoing research continues to identify the benefits and mechanism of individual creativity. A laundry list of benefits that includes:

☐ Resilience

☐ Happiness

☐ Job performance improvement

☐ Job satisfaction rises

☐ Salary opportunities

☐ Adaptability and agility despite uncertainty

☐ Effective leadership

☐ Innovation

☐ Profitability

☐ Talent attraction and retention

☐ Team cohesion

☐ Innovation

☐ And on and on and on.

These benefits are accessible to those with the willingness to walk their own plank and then leap.

What is your storyline for creativity facing adversity and challenges? It's yours to write. And you can rewrite it, you know, without scary clowns. Just get creative. The first step? Choose to take a tiny, insignificant risk today. Then, imagine what you could do if you were comfortable taking many tiny risks that together could add up to bold, substantial impact on your family, your industry, your life?

Yes, each tiny risk may seem inconsequential. Yet, each tiny risk helps you build strength and personal creative resilience.

- Toss in that extra dash of chili powder in the recipe.

- Try out a new shortcut to the store.

- Wear something you like instead of what others do.

- Listen to a podcast on a topic you know nothing about.

- Share your appreciation for a co-worker.

But Did You DIE?

This could be your new mantra for facing new experiences. If you can ask yourself that question, then things are just fine. Because...if you can't ask yourself that question you are either dead or unconscious which are both fairly serious.

If you practice rebounding from failure in a creative endeavour, you will learn how to rebound from life's other failures. Exercising creativity is like going to the gym to build your resilience muscles.

If you still think that creativity is overrated, or fluff for kids and grandmas, then stop reading now. Maybe you need some counselling instead. Might I suggest an art therapist? The next chapters are chock full of everyday creativity.

3

Just Tell Me How to Get To
EVERYDAY CREATIVITY

The real reason you're here: *what can you do to engage your everyday creativity?*

Maybe you pride yourself on having an "Inbox Zero." That's cool. I can't help you there. Except that by engaging your creativity, you might discover a great new way to get there. All you have to do is **D.A.N.C.E.** This is my acronym for the five things you can do in minutes a day to welcome your own, unique style of creativity into your day. These techniques work regardless of your personality, culture, or creative outlet.

If you are reading this book because people say that you need to be creative and you don't know how, Chapters Four through Eight explain an effortless habit for each letter in the **D.A.N.C.E.** acronym to engage your creativity every day, in only five minutes.

Want the abridged version? Tear out the next page and tape it to your computer or download the PDF from under Ch. 3 at thereluctantcreative.com/resources[12] as a visual reminder each day. If you resist one of the strategies, you probably expect me to tell you to only do the ones that you like. Heck no! This is a story about challenging your comfort zone, building resilience, and doing the hard things. Do the one that you resist most *FIRST*.

For those who need a bit more foreplay, let's explore the creative process. How can you set up an environment and mindset to succeed? What kinds of creativity are there, and do they need different conditions? Isn't there just a colour I can paint on my walls to get inspired?

---

12   D.A.N.C.E. Download available at thereluctantcreative.com/resources

D — DAYDREAM

A — AMBIGUITY

N — NOVELTY

C — CURIOSITY

E — EDIT LATER

The Creative Difference

Creativity needs space and time. Employees need to have the room to find flow to perform with creativity. Building an environment for creativity seems to fly in the face of any attempts to be "productive." Steve Jobs knew this. Einstein knew this. Now you know it, too.

There are two main types of creative thinking, each with their own unique requirements for success. Knowing these will help you **D.A.N.C.E.** with more confidence and impact.

1. **Divergent Creativity** — "anything is possible" creativity. "What if" thinking with no clear answer or outcome.

2. **Convergent Creativity** — one specific answer through creativity. For example, finding the "right" word for a poem.

People sometimes think that all creativity involves divergent thinking. *Divergent creativity* is brainstorming, improvisation, and discovering big ideas. If you were writing a poem, divergent thinking involves dreaming up ideas about what to write about, characters, and theme. If you were in a product development meeting, divergent thinking would be used to come up with a huge list of possibilities for your next launch. Divergent thinking works best in a physical place that feels open, connected with nature, possibly in a blue or green room, furniture with rounded edges, sometimes with dim lighting, and with diverse working areas for collaboration like white boards or chalkboards.

Convergent creativity helps you prune out the bad ideas and start zooming in on the ones that you want to develop. Yes, there are bad ideas. Honegar remedy (combine honey/vinegar), electrified water baths for hangovers, and Troll Dolls come to mind (all three have existed in the marketplace). If you were writing a poem, convergent creativity would help you find that exact right phrase for your poem. If you were in a meeting, converging helps to determine which product idea will move forward to test and develop.

Convergent thinking often works best in a more focused and somber environment, and many people find it easier to converge alone. We'll be diving deeper into divergent and convergent thinking in Chapter Eight — E. is for Edit Later, the critical habit you need if you want to create better and more useful ideas.

There are many frameworks to use creativity more effectively. Creative Problem Solving and Design Thinking give a proven structure to identify the real problem and take it through a framework to identify steps for solutions. Facilitators skilled in these methods help organizations avoid pitfalls of jumping too quickly to solutions, and not articulating the challenge properly.

According to Anthony Brandt and David Eagleman in Time magazine's Special Edition on Creativity, creative ideas fall into three main categories:

1. Breaking

2. Blending

3. Bending

Genetics Professor Randy Lewis used blending when he imagined that ultra-strong silk could make an ultralight bullet proof vest. However, farming spiders became (understandably) problematic, if not perilous. Maybe he's the same guy who tried to figure out how to herd cats. Instead of trying to figure out how to farm spiders more effectively, he blended the idea of silk production with a different source, a goat. Randy spliced the silk producing DNA into Freckles the goat, who secretes spider silk in her milk. Fusion cuisine is another example of blending; Japanese American, Tex-Mex, or Indo-Chinese.

Breaking involves taking a concept and separating all the individual pieces to build something new. Mosaics are an example of breaking pottery and reassembling the pieces into a new work of art.

Bending is an adaptation of a theme. One could adapt with size, shape, or function. Imagine taking the concept of electrolyte transfer through a cell and use the concept in car design. Or perhaps making miniature windmills for small voltage energy generation.

A key point is that originality is not a precursor to creativity. People often believe that to be creative, it must be completely original.

CREATIVITY IS PLAGIARISM, UNDISCOVERED.

Earlier, we met Natasha Purnell, whose creative ideas to engage her team are not new, but she applied them in unique ways to her organization.

If you can identify the type of creativity that you need for each situation, you can adapt your environment and processes to support, instead of hinder, the creative process required at each stage. If you try to diverge and converge at the same time, you'll end up at a standstill. Isn't there just a magic paint chip to catalyze innovation and creative thinking?

Creative Environments for Collaboration

Since everyone has a different style of creativity, what sparks ideas is as different as our individual fingerprints. There has been some research on the types of physical environments that can improve creative thinking in most people. Many of the ways to improve a physical environment for creativity are the same as techniques to improve comfort, health, and safety.

Unfortunately, there are no "rose coloured creativity glasses" to magically engage creativity. However, some themes have consistently shown a positive influence on organizational or individual creativity. As noted earlier, diversity in the workforce has been shown to increase creativity, leading to increased organizational innovation.

Leadership support for creativity, combined with HR creativity initiatives have also been positive drivers of individual creativity in organizations.

Individual creativity is heavily influenced by one's mood. Low activity states, being tired and sleepy, or angry or sad, hamper individual creativity. Happier states with a more positive energy are historically correlated with creativity. Some research contends that the most creative states come from a state of ambivalence, where positive and negative states are experienced simultaneously. New research on students during COVID are finding an interesting link between depression and creativity. In students with strong emotional resilience, depression is a catalyst to apply creative thinking to improve their mood and prospects.

Building on the work of Ruth Richards' everyday creativity and the common factors required for a creative environment, certain environmental designs for schools have been proposed to be more conducive to creativity. Environments should allow independent work, be stimulating but not distracting, and allow easy access to resources. The school findings align well with those in the organizational setting.

Creativity in organizations foundationally requires psychological safety. Since everyone is creative, it makes sense that the environment for creativity is what dictates individual creativity. Can't we just outsource this whole she-bang to someone else? It sounds hard.

Nope! Individual creativity relies on the fundamental condition that we will be safe when we share our ideas with the world. On an individual level, it requires an override button to that outdated survival instinct, creative enemy #2 — judgement from others.

Sorry to disappoint. A paint colour or a screensaver solution would have been much easier. All this psychological safety and reserved judgment is hard stuff. Never fear, though, as there are some physical adaptions that may help. Let's explore!

Creative Spaces

A creative space often conjures up a Google-inspired open concept building with lots of windows, free food, ping pong tables, singalong spaces and nap pods. Steve Jobs deliberately designed the offices at Pixar to encourage random collaboration. One bathroom block for the whole complex, complete with blackboards for random thoughts, allowed for random connections and a way to articulate random ideas. Circular boardroom desks encouraged discussion and removed the physical hierarchy from meetings to allow more exchange of ideas. The typical brainstorming session brings to mind an engaged group of extroverts, shouting out inspiration and writing brilliant ideas down on a white board. Yet, 70% of people say they would rather create alone.

Some people believe that employees would rather feel appreciated and valued by their organizations than have free lunch or a ping pong table. I suspect that this effect will be the same for creativity — physical environmental changes may increase creativity but will be fruitless without the basic necessities of psychological safety and support for experimentation and innovative exploration.

The following is a list of physical environment adaptations that have been shown to influence creativity:

1. **Personalized workspace** — 32% of employees who could personalize their space were more productive.

2. **Furniture** — Rounded furniture can improve collective mindset and belonging and increase divergent thinking. Angular furniture can facilitate convergent, more focused thinking.

3. **Lighting** — Dim lighting has long been suggested to help with divergent creativity. Like rounded furniture, dim lighting is helpful for idea generation, but bright lighting is helpful for analytical and convergent thinking. Dim light might also support the practice of limiting the visual part of our brain when we are working on an insight or bright idea. Why lighting? Imagine an off the wall idea, then imagine the face of your manager when you tell them. There is less fear of judgement if you can't see the nuanced judgement on someone's face. I doubt I'm the only one

who has spilled my guts out to a friend while camping under the stars or talk about things that were otherwise uncomfortable under the safety of lights out at a sleepover. Here's another business idea. Instead of rose-coloured glasses, there should be blackout glasses. Rose coloured, sure, when you want to feel happy, but with a blackout function when you want to be creative. Not unlike the glasses that Zaphod Beeblebrox wears in *The Hitchhiker's Guide to the Galaxy*[13] which black out when something dangerous is near, so he doesn't have to be scared.

4. **Space** — High ceilings and bright natural light are thought to foster feelings of freedom, which are helpful for creativity. Another study found that narrow, restrictive spaces made people feel confined. The desire to escape confinement spurred varied and unique, creative choices. So, who really knows on that one? Conclusion pending. Perhaps the narrow space was more influential on creative ideas through constraints and urgency, instead of a physical space factor.

5. **Nature and Biophilia** — *the urge to affiliate with other forms of life.* Use the pickup line, "Are you feeling biophilic" at your peril, unless you are at a mixer for evolutionary psychologists. Plants lower stress, prevent fatigue, and restore attention, which are all positive mindsets to creativity. The benefits are also realized

---

13 *The Hitchhiker's Guide to the Galaxy* by Douglas Adams

when looking at a screensaver or out a window if you don't have a green thumb. Plants and nature are healing and soothing to the senses. In patients recovering from surgery, recovery was faster if their view out of the window included trees. I have not seen any research on having dead plants around, but my guess is that a picture of a live plant is probably better than a dead plant.

6. **Saccadic Eye Movements** — rapid eye movements to scan the environment are also a tool for engaging creativity. As Donald Rattner explains in his book, *My Creative Space: How to Design Your Home, Stimulate Ideas, and Spark Innovation,* looking to the left stimulates the right hemisphere, and vice versa. Organic views, like looking at a forest or garden, are more irregular than a more manufactured or homogeneous view. Natural environments stimulate more eye movement and since creativity is a whole brain exercise, these eye movements help to promote creative thinking. Throw that one into your yoga routine!

7. **Messy Desk** — I think I know what happened here. In a lab or office, there are always people who have a messy desk and are chastised by their coworkers. Hands up, that's me! Apparently, the messy desk folks all got together and vindicated themselves with research that suggests that a messy desk helps creativity,

and they would be right. More importantly, the study authors do not identify who had the messy desk, and how excited they were to rub the research in their collaborator's faces that their messy desk is a good thing. As a counterpoint, orderly desks can also be a good thing, if you are chasing healthy lifestyles, larger donations to support your organization's goals, and status quo solutions.

"IF A CLUTTERED DESK IS A SIGN OF A CLUTTERED MIND, OF WHAT, THEN, IS AN EMPTY DESK A SIGN?"

—Albert Einstein

8. **Colours** — Here's our paint chip! Blue has positive effects on creativity, due to "approach motivation," whereas red stimulates "avoidance motivation," which is best for tasks requiring focused attention and details. When we are motivated by avoiding something

negative (avoidance motivation), we focus on details, our thinking becomes more rigid, and we struggle to see the big picture. Approach motivation is more open, more "forest than the tree-ish." Since cultural views towards colours are so diverse, this could be an effect unique to specific cultures, so worth more investigation.

9. **Taste** — Grandma had the right idea with her tiny bowl of candies. Sweet tastes contributed the most to creative thinking.

10. **Physical Movement** — Physically connecting to a metaphor for creativity, such as actually sitting next to a box (to generate "out of the box ideas"), walking aimlessly and using body movements, all have positive impacts on creativity. With the rise of "sitting is the new smoking" health issues, having the ability to get up and move around or working at a standing desk are not only creative drivers but positive for general health and well-being. In a very comprehensive look at adapting physical environments for creativity, Donald Rattner contends in his book, *My Creative Space*, that "Any mechanism that can lift us out of our ass-magnets for even a few hours a day has to benefit our health, our brains, and our butts." Truer words have never been spoken. While at my standing desk, reading this chapter in my own Creative Space, I could

not help but feel a bit smug. I celebrated my success with a milkshake. I know, I'm a work in progress. For more details on adapting a physical space to promote creativity, I highly recommend *My Creative Space* by Donald Rattner.

4

D. is for DAYDREAM

La-la land. Navel Gazing. Dreamland. Wool-Gathering. Head in the Clouds. Space Cadet. Out to lunch. Castle-Building.

Our first foray into **D.A.N.C.E.** is **Daydream** — the beautiful power of letting our mind wander.

Daydreaming has a bad Public Relations team. Most expressions for "daydreaming" don't sound very fun, or useful. Except castle building which sounds very Type A, overachieving and suitably important, but perhaps not particularly useful today.

When you are doing "nothing," your brain is working overtime, you just can't feel it. If you were in a functional MRI (fMRI) where we could see what areas of your brain are active, scientists would see an active brain, highlighting the Default Mode Network (DMN). Such a boring name for such a ground-breaking discovery — that when you feel like you are doing nothing, areas of your brain that don't normally communicate get together for a neurobiological keg party. Doing nothing could actually be doing everything.

J.K. Rowling discovered the benefits of daydreaming while on a stalled train in London. Lacking a smartphone, book, magazine, or Rubik's Cube, she stared out the window. While daydreaming, she created the storyline for the entire Harry Potter series. It took years of development, writing and painstaking editing (and converging!) to create the books we love today. But it started with a daydream.

Galileo, bored at church, watched the candelabras high above in the cathedral swing back and forth. Curious, he started timing the swing to his pulse. Eventually, his daydreaming about candelabras led to pendulum theory, and the discovery of clocks many decades later.

DMN — Daydream (Default) Mode Network

When researchers discovered the paradoxically active brain while daydreaming, they dubbed it the *Default Mode Network (DMN)*. The discovery was, like many things in science, a total accident.

Dr. Randy Buckner studied the brains of people performing a task-based activity. He then planned to scan the brains of hapless college students, to compare two tasks to see what part of the brain was involved in each. As a good researcher, Dr. Buckner wanted a "control" state, so he did what made the most sense. To compare two tasks where you are actively "doing something," a reasonable control would be to "do nothing." It was the "doing nothing" part that ended up being labeled the DMN — not by Dr. Buckner, but by Dr. Marcus Raichle and his team, pulling together decades of research.

But, since we're dealing with the brain, things are not always simple. The DMN is not only used in passive states, but it's also active in other contexts. We are constantly learning more about our brain and how it works[14]. We're so smart, because of our big brains, how could we ever hope to be smart enough to understand this high level of complexity?

Productive Boredom

Boredom sucks. It's literally in the definition.

> "an unpleasant, transient affective state in which the individual feels a pervasive lack of interest in and difficulty concentrating on the current activity ... [such that] it takes conscious effort to maintain or return attention to that activity."

Trust scientists as the only people who can make boredom...more boring.

---

14 For a super fun and nerdy detour, check out this YouTube video with Alan Alda and Dr. Raichle about the DMN under Ch. 3 at thereluctantcreative.com/resources

Boredom results when we can't engage with our environment, even if we want to. The negative state of boredom launches us out of what we are doing that feels boring, into something else. The gift of boredom helps us to learn self awareness of our goals, desires, and values. We don't stop being bored by simply changing things up. Boredom resolves only when we find an activity that is more aligned with our plans and wishes.

BOREDOM'S FUNCTION, THEN, IS BASICALLY TO KICK YOUR ASS BACK TO WHAT MATTERS.

Imagine counting dandelions in a field. Personally, I would find that quite boring. Would you? But, for some reason, let's say you had to. Boredom incites our attention to shift from the boring task of counting dandelions (external focus) to seek stimulation from our own thoughts and feelings (inner focus). This inner focus is what we call "daydreaming." During the daydreaming state, we can use dynamic memory (a fancy word for imagining alternate endings) to rewrite the script around situations and problems in our life. Daydreaming is like a virtual reality Groundhog Day. Not the day, but the movie with Bill Murray where he repeats the day over and over again. Go watch it if you haven't seen it. Go ahead. In fact, I think I'll go watch it myself!

Boredom researchers Sandi Mann and Rebekah Cadman decided to bore participants in different ways. They found higher creativity in people who were bored, mainly from a task involving reading (vs. writing).

DOES THE IRONY NOT ESCAPE ANYONE ELSE THAT IT TAKES **MASSIVE CREATIVITY** TO DESIGN A TASK THAT CAN BORE PEOPLE IN JUST THE RIGHT WAY?

Boredom is another state, like discomfort, that we avoid at all costs. Smartphones have let us easily avoid the discomfort of boredom. We hate boredom so much that in one surprisingly recent, very ethically dodgy-sounding experiment, subjects preferred to self-administer electric shocks to themselves rather than sit alone with their thoughts.

There is a lot more to the science of boredom, relating to high and low arousal and mental health connections, I'm just showing you the entrance to the rabbit hole. As we will discuss later in Chapter Five — A. is for Ambiguity, people often have a similar negative reaction to boredom as when faced with feelings of uncertainty.

Remember Adam Grant's TED Talk about flow being a predictor of happiness during the pandemic? Boredom can create a state of disengagement, whereas flow is a state of hyper-engagement.

But boredom is not all bad. Productive Boredom is what I call the good kind of boredom, which involves daydreaming with the anchor being something interesting, or a problem you want to solve[15]. Unproductive boredom involves ruminating on the look the waitress gave you at lunch. A new study links daydreaming to creativity, but only the type of daydreaming that involves fantastical and fictional imagination, as compared to "why did I send that email" and "why didn't I get any zucchini in my garden this year?"

"EUREKA!!!" By Design

Daydreaming is often a precursor to a massive insight, like the cliché story about Archimedes who allegedly jumped out of the tub in the inaugural Eureka! moment when he discovered the theory of buoyancy. Creative ideas often appear

---

15 If you are bored, check out thereluctantcreative.com/resources and explore all the interviews, links and worksheets.

while performing a cognitively undemanding task, like driving a car or having a shower. Shannon from WaitWell, who we met in Chapter One, gets her insights when walking her dog. Other famous walking thinkers include Steve Jobs, Albert Einstein, Darwin and more. During an undemanding task, we keep our analytical brain just busy enough to allow our minds to wander, leading to more creative ideas. If you've ever looked closely at someone about to solve a problem with an insight, you might have noticed a few mannerisms. They might look up at the sky, squint while pinching the bridge of their nose, or shield the eyes with a hand. Immediately, before we leap out of the bathtub in a "Eureka!" moment, our brain makes us temporarily blind, to allow us to focus on the brilliance striking our brain like lightning. In fact, if you are hooked up to an EEG to monitor your brain waves, the researcher can see that you are going to have an insight moments before you actually have it. Possibly a new smartphone app or life hack?

Researchers suggest that we get more insights in the shower because it decreases visual stimulation, as well as keeps our inner critic busy with a menial but not all-absorbing task. I think I get insights in there because it's the only place I can sing without getting yelled at.

If you are trying to solve a problem requiring an "aha" or insight, then mind wandering, or daydreaming, is a good strategy (remember divergent creativity). However, if you are trying to solve a problem requiring analytical thought, then mindfulness and focused attention is important (think convergent creativity).

Mindfulness impairs intuitive thinking or spontaneous insights — which makes sense if we use daydreaming to achieve insight or intuition. Remember, daydreaming is the act of thinking about different scenarios and building different stories. Mindfulness is the practice of being completely in the moment, not dreaming about possibilities, but of experiencing the present.

Mindfulness can paradoxically help us get back on track. Mindfulness may not directly improve creativity, but it can alter our ability to think differently. Kerryn Fewster, an expert on Tolerance of Ambiguity (more on this is Chapter Five), notes that mindfulness can calm our instinctive negative response to change, disruption, or ambiguity. With a calm mental frame of mind, we can engage our logical thinking part of our brain to work out a way forward. We learn to sit in ambiguity instead of immediately fretting about the future. Mindfulness creates space for creativity by allowing us to sit in the moment as we explore, experiment, and get curious, instead of blurting out an unconscious reaction.

Your mind has probably wandered a few times while reading this book. Estimates suggest that we spend 30-50% of our waking consciousness daydreaming. In many cases, mind wandering is associated with a lower mood. Can you remember a time you ruminated over a misstep? Like that time you confused the Spanish for "Blonde" (Rubio) with "Red" (Roja) in a taxi in Costa Rica, when you were trying to confidently ask "What is that red glow over there" and, instead apparently asked "What is that blonde over there?" while driving on a dark road in the middle of the night near a volcano. Or the time you quipped "love you" to your boss as you hung up the phone. No? Just me?

However, our mood improves in instances where mind-wandering is focused on something that we find interesting. In these cases, mind-wandering is associated with future planning and creativity, which makes sense. It is way more interesting to imagine walking on the red carpet at the Oscars when your book has been made into a hit movie starring Meryl Streep and Robert DeNiro...sorry where was I? Oh yes, mind wandering about interesting and fantastical futures instead of daydreaming about zucchini.

If you find yourself ruminating instead of daydreaming, you might go for a walk, do something, *anything*, different, then return to daydreaming when you are in a more relaxed frame of mind. So, if we target our daydreaming to specific subjects, not only can it help to find new solutions, but it can also lift our mood. From an organizational perspective, daydreaming is inevitable. If you want daydreaming team or family members to advance your goals, encourage daydreaming about something of interest, instead of perilous ruminating over excessively cc'd emails and memos on break room hygiene.

1, 2, 3, DAYDREAM! Keep Your Critic Busy

Remember the inner mean critic (mine is Todd) who uses logic and rational arguments to keep you small and safe? Let's give that critic something better to do!

In divergent thinking and problems requiring insight, our biggest obstacle is our inner critic. If we can cleverly trick our analytical brain into focusing on something else, but not so much that it requires our full attention, it leaves our Default Mode Network to wander and play. It's kind of like opening the Tupperware cabinet to occupy a baby so that you can make dinner. The best environment for daydreaming is often found in nature and while doing another task. If you can't find nature, even images of nature on a screen are conducive to creativity.

Channel your inner 19th century **French Flaneur** — a term used to describe a wealthy man who would walk around town as his primary occupation. While "Flaneur" is unlikely to be one of the 97M new jobs in 2025, there is something brilliant about walking with no intention, no agenda, and being open to the experience. Many famous writers, thinkers and scientists embraced the idea of wandering without an agenda and credited this practice for their success.

Paul Gavarni, Le Flâneur, 1842.

"THOSE WHO
DREAM BY DAY
ARE COGNIZANT OF
MANY THINGS WHICH
ESCAPE THOSE WHO
DREAM ONLY
BY NIGHT."

—Edgar Allan Poe

Daydream Dare

Think about a problem you are trying to solve.

_____

_____

Now, look out the window or find a nature scene on your phone and jot down any thoughts or images that pop up.

 (Video: Daydream Dare*)

Remember:

1. Don't try to solve the problem. Think about the problem and let your mind wander

2. Don't edit your thoughts. If your brain wants to wander to Beverly Hills, let it go, jot it down, and don't judge.

3. Set a timer for 5 minutes or more.

*Find the video and a PDF download of this sheet at thereluctantcreative.com/resources

Wander Dare

Go for a wanderer and take notes. Sketch something you see. Put a few items on your wander between these pages to keep. Notice what happens to the item and the pages over time. ▶ (Video: Wander Dare*)

What did you see?

Name 3 things you noticed.

Tape a treasure you found here. →

More on the next page

What surprised you?

_____

_____

_____

Sketch something here.

5

A ∘ is for AMBIGUITY

The girl slapped the boy on the horse.

This is an ambiguous sentence. Were they both on the horse? Or was the boy on the horse, and the girl on the ground? What is all the slapping about? And why is the horse putting up with all this crap?

Ambiguity and Uncertainty

Ambiguity is merely a situation that presents more than one meaning.

Uncertainty is our emotion or state in response to ambiguity. Remember the uncertainty of March 2020, and the predictions of temporary setbacks, now laughable in hindsight? While it was novel to find ourselves suddenly working from home in the first weeks of the COVID pandemic, as the months progressed, we collectively faced massive ambiguity. This ambiguity led many to question their sanity, to grasp at baseless predictions that suited their narrative, and to struggle to find the energy to do much more than get out of bed in the morning. Uncertainty is crippling.

We have developed a sweet tooth for certainty that is often operating at an unconscious level. Certainty afforded us survival. We have developed responses to uncertainty to move us towards action, and these responses are usually something that has worked for us in the past. Our world is changing so rapidly that we can't rely on outdated evolutionary survival instincts any longer.

I remember a time I felt very uncertain and experienced the lure of the status quo. I was about nine years old and wanted to go sledding. Nobody else could go and I didn't want to walk to the sledding hill a few blocks away. Luckily, I lived at the bottom of a street on a huge hill. Genius, I thought, I'll just sled down the pavement. Keep in mind that I was only nine, for crying out loud! I hauled my large wooden sled to the top of the hill, gripping the pathetic piece of twine at the front of the sled in my mittened hands. I used the twine to pull the sled up the hill, but it was also used as a false rudder, giving an illusion of control as I hurtled down the hill. Anyone who has hurtled down the hill on one of those old wooden toboggans knows that the twine does nothing to turn anything (this is important... in a second. Keep going). So, there I was, on the sidewalk at the top of my street. This was new! What a great idea, I thought! Remember, I was NINE and clueless. I pushed off, down the hill. I started to accelerate, faster and faster.

Suddenly, I realized the perilous fate looming
ahead of me on the busy street which crossed
at the end of my road. The one I was currently
hurtling down. I also realized that I had forgotten to secure the twine, which was stubbornly
dragging under the speeding toboggan. I was out of control.

What could I do? Should I jump off, use my feet to
slow the toboggan down, cry for help, what else? I was in
the worst situation, feeling uncertain with massive urgency
and perilous stakes. What would you have done? I'll let
you simmer for a moment in the uncertainty. Apparently,
this is a storytelling trick, to delay the story ending, which
naturally keeps our attention — our addiction to certainty
is responsible for the use of the "cliff hanger."

Today, our speeding toboggans are emails, politics, the
Internet, relationships, school forms, and if you're anything
like me, laundry. In addition to uncertainty feeling unpleasant, it affects the way we make decisions. In one study, two
groups were each shown a set of playing cards. One set of
cards was normal (yay, a control!) and the other contained
ambiguous cards, where some of the red suits were black
and vice-versa. Before and after the experiment, the participants were asked to share their feelings on affirmative
action. It is important to know that the group who were
shown the weird cards did not even notice that the card
colours were wrong, so this effect was unconscious. The
group shown the ambiguous cards were more likely to cling
to their previously held beliefs, and less open to considering

an alternative point of view than the group who were shown the normal cards. Unconscious bias, much?

Uncertainty is sneaky. Much like the subjects who were shown the ambiguous cards without recognizing them, we can be completely unaware that we are feeling uncertain. When faced with ambiguity, our brain kicks into "data collection" mode, scanning the environment for clues. Once we have collected relevant information, we are pushed into making a decision. Usually that decision is a strategy that has worked for us in the past. So, although we might logically reason that we need new solutions to tackle today's problems, our biology pushes us to status quo thinking. After all, it's what got us here in the first place, right?

Now knowing how we react to uncertainty what do you think I did on that toboggan that was hurtling me towards a grisly fate? Well, I did not do any of the things that would have made sense (again, remember that I was only nine).

Any other time I had been on this toboggan, when I made it to the bottom alive, I had been holding on to the illusion of control with the twine. In the panicked urgency of hurtling down the hill, I did what researchers have said we do in uncertainty. I jumped to a status quo solution, one which had worked for me in the past. I leaned over the front of the toboggan that was hurtling down the hill and tried to pull the twine out from under the moving toboggan. Well, it wasn't that disastrous because I didn't die, and it laughably worked to avoid the busy intersection. But I did get a bloody nose from the impact of a toboggan smashing into my face. Because...physics. Maybe this explains why I dropped Freshman Physics multiple times.

The world is throwing ambiguity at us like elves throwing rice at a wedding. Why elves? I don't know. I picture elves as frantic and over-enthusiastic rice throwers. Apologies to the chill and relaxed elves out there.

Ironically, we are getting less and less comfortable with ambiguity, thanks to our "Google it" culture of always having the answers at our fingertips. We don't even seem to care if it is the right answer, either.

Sitting in ambiguity, despite the discomfort, allows us to imagine multiple possible storylines, instead of jumping to a status-quo solution. Mindfulness allows us to stay present, in the discomfort, to feel more comfortable with the grey space of the unknown. In that space, we can imagine other possibilities, using our divergent thinking to explore "what if" thinking.

As a veterinarian, I experience this effect all the time. Jonesy the cat might have thrown up once yesterday and has some diarrhea today. After determining that Jonesy seems stable, her owners want to know what happened. We can't ask Jonesy, but we can explore possible stories. I could create 150 different plausible stories for why Jonesy got an upset tummy. Now, imagine that Jonesy's owners tell me that they found a chocolate wrapper on the floor. We grasp at this answer because it "makes sense" and it appeases our need for certainty. But if we write the tantalizing taste of chocolate certainty in ink, we might lose sight of other possibilities.

At the end of the day, we will probably never find out. Even with all the tests in the world. And sometimes, that's what happens — we go chasing certainty with medical tests. This happens in human medicine too and is termed "overdiagnosis," leading to discovery of irrelevant medical issues or spurious results that have physicians chasing waterfalls. Physicians with a need to run every test are seeking certainty and are less resilient with a lower tolerance for ambiguity. And TLC was pretty clear about not "chasing waterfalls" in the '90s, and I believe it is still sound advice today[16].

Great, so what does that all have to do with creativity?

All Creativity is Uncertain

Let's say that again —

ALL CREATIVITY IS UNCERTAIN.

To engage in any creative process is to face uncertainty and failure. If we can learn to identify and get curious about our feelings of uncertainty, instead of being a slave to the reaction, to resist the shove towards status quo solutions, we can seek novel and pertinent solutions that better suit our challenges today. How will we get better at identifying and addressing our feelings of uncertainty? Practice, of course, just like with failure and judgement.

---

16 For you TLC fans — find a link to a nostalgic detour under Ch. 5 at thereluctantcreative.com/resources

Building our tolerance of ambiguity allows us to imagine a different path, a different future.

Tolerance of Ambiguity

Tolerance of Ambiguity (TOA) is a typical research-ey phrase. TOA is how much you freak out (or not) in a situation that does not have a clear answer or solution. A hostage negotiator is usually fairly tolerant. They are adept at sitting around for five days in the desert, taking their time, with the highest of stakes in play. When we are not comfortable with ambiguity, we seek closure. The famous Waco cult standoff dragged on for days. Finally, the military supervisor got tired of the hostage negotiator's tactics and stormed the facilities, resulting in tragic loss of life. Sadly, it seemed that the group had been getting ready to turn themselves in. Or more simply, remember that time you had a fight with your high school sweetheart, and you couldn't stand the insecurity anymore, so you make a late-night panicked call to just end it already? No? Just me?

You might know someone who has to check out a menu online before agreeing to a restaurant choice or must know the result of the game as soon as it happens, or dictates lunch and break schedules to professional employees. We've all encountered these individuals who tend to have a lower tolerance for ambiguity.

Kerryn Fewster and Peter O'Connor looked at TOA specifically in the workplace. Although they did not identify a causal relationship, TOA correlated highly with resilience and creativity. If you could practice, improve, or build upon TOA, creativity or resilience, could you then potentially increase the others? Sadly, although it would conveniently support my cry to creative arms, correlation is not causation. Here is your Public Service Announcement for critical thinking: examples of other correlations are ice cream leads to murder, or Mexican lemon imports prevent highway deaths[17].

You might already know if you tolerate uncertainty more than most people. If you don't, or you love quizzes, Fewster with AdaptIQ Minds, one of the researchers from the TOA workplace study, has a quiz (yay for a quiz that takes the ambiguity out of how much ambiguity you have!)[18].

Having a high TOA is correlated to a wide array of benefits to individuals and organizations. Benefits include better complex problem solving, critical thinking, creativity, job satisfaction, risk acceptance, health and wellbeing, effective leadership, higher job performance and lower staff turnover.

Other studies have extolled the virtues of being comfortable with ambiguity, especially as it relates to mental wellness. In 2019, a systematic review of many studies determined that TOA is associated with psychological well-being. A little tip here is that if you don't love reading tons of studies like me, look for a "systematic review" article which is basically a lazy way to have a really smart person

---

17 Don't believe me? Check it out under Ch. 5 at thereluctantcreative.com/resources
18 Find the snapshot assessment under Ch. 5 at thereluctantcreative.com/resources

evaluate a bunch of studies and tell you whether it's BS or brilliant, without having to evaluate the statistical method. Physicians are a group with a high degree of stress and anxiety, and with a wide variation in their TOA. Those with a high need for closure, low TOA, and less years in practice were significantly predicted to suffer from work-related stress. Now, while TOA might seem like a magic bullet, there can be a downside. Physicians with a high TOA might have a high degree of comfort in acting despite having all the answers, which can lead to quick fixes and lazy decisions, which are also not in the patient's best interest. Curiosity is a corrective factor for physicians with both high and low tolerance of ambiguity to make better decisions. We'll learn more about Curiosity in Chapter Seven — C. is for Curiosity.

Imagine this real-life scenario: I'm working in the Operating Room with my colleague, Mary (not her real name), who is a phenomenal veterinarian, and (I suspect to be) less tolerant of ambiguity than me. We are standing over a dog who has been hit by a car and has a pneumothorax (extra air around the lungs preventing him from breathing). He needs a chest tube. Mary starts counting the ribs to find the correct landmark, stops to check vitals, clips the hair a little bit wider. My eyes are bugging out of my head as I am restraining myself from just SLAMMING THE CHEST TUBE IN RIGHT NOW. I was curious, but more in a "WHAT IS TAKING YOU SO LONG" instead of a more productive curiosity which would be "what could we be missing here?" We made a great team, because her painstaking and thorough approach kept me from moving too fast, and my tolerance of ambiguity nudged her along to act in a reasonable time.

Based on what we know about uncertainty's effects on decision making, which is to push us to status quo solutions, it makes sense that an ability to sit with uncertainty leads to more innovative and creative decisions. So, what influences TOA? Genetics, so far, can't change those, and personality—specifically openness to experience, layered with life experience, intent, and practice. This we can change, but it's hard.

Researchers have identified some ways you can increase your own TOA:

1. **Art Appreciation.** Medical students who participated in an art appreciation course had higher TOA. Interestingly, these students also had a significant increase in empathy.

2. **Uncertainty Training.** In a group of MS patients, a six-week program focused on learning and discussion around uncertainty vs control resulted in increased TOA, as well as acceptance of their diagnosis.

3. **Collaboration and Engagement.** In Greece, a public sector railway organization successfully introduced a knowledge management model that resulted in both increased TOA as well as productivity, in a population that was particularly averse to ambiguity.

4. **Workplace TOA.** The Fewster/O'Connor[19] study
explored TOA specifically in the workplace, in a corporate setting, to determine what factors might help
employees and leaders with uncertainty. Eight principles emerged from the data, which you can practice
to increase your TOA even if you are an unapologetic
certainty chaser. The most highly correlated factors
with Tolerance of Ambiguity were Resilience and
Creativity.

   i.   Master Mindfulness

   ii. Be Assertive

   iii. Focus on What Matters

   iv. Practice Agility

   v.   Cultivate Curiosity

   vi. Act Courageously

   vii. Let Go and Move On

   viii.Think Differently (which is basically creativity)

Today, take a few minutes to identify how your body
and mind responds to uncertainty. A mindfulness practice
will help. I'm not talking about meditating on a bed of nails
in a thong. Mindfulness means to take the time to immerse
yourself in the present moment. Try chewing a piece of food

---

19 Find an interview with Kerryn Fewster for more on TOA under Ch. 5 at
thereluctantcreative.com/resources

to enjoy the texture and taste, instead of searching for the next bite on your plate. Look at the flower by the path and really see it, explore the symmetry of the petals, the exquisite detail in the pollen, instead of rushing to Starbucks. Colour or doodle in a notebook (or the margins of this book!). Enjoy the feeling of sand on your toes instead of mentally planning your next vacation. Over time, with awareness, you can learn to delay a decision as much as possible. Allow your good old frontal cortex to get in on the action, so to speak.

For example, my physical response to ambiguity is the same every time, whether my name is called to step on stage, I'm standing at the top of a challenging ski run, making a new recipe, or writing a chapter in my book. I often get these same physical feelings when faced with my process for creative resistance, as I described on pages 56–57. I feel like I want to bounce on the balls of my feet, I have a sensation of watching a tennis match, flip flopping back and forth, and I want to shake out my hands. I get tension around my mouth and my vision seems to narrow in focus. I work on trying to be aware when I feel this way, so that my uncertainty is more conscious. This awareness allows my big brain to step in and calm down my panicking minions who are trying to solve the problem without really knowing what they are solving in the first place.

Considering the benefits of creativity such as job satisfaction, higher salary, and an overall better mood, it's like a mega bonus that one helps the other. Creativity and ambiguity are a pair of superheroes, helping you find better jobs, feel better, and take more chances to expand your comfort zone to become a better human.

It helps that they also look good in tights.

How does uncertainty make you feel?

Connect the dots

Don't overthink it. Start connecting the dots and let your mind tell you where to go.

What did you draw?
It can be a thing, feeling, or something else.

Surprising Stories

Write one word for each:

1. Adjective _____

2. Verb _____

3. Noun, item _____

4. Job _____

5. Verb _____

6. Animal _____

7. Verb _____

8. Animal _____

9. Verb _____

Now, go to the next page and fill in the blanks.

It was a (1) _____ day.

She (2) _____ into the store,

looking for a (3) _____.

The (4) _____ asked her what

she was (5) _____ for. Suddenly,

a (6) _____ burst into the

store and started (7) _____ the

shelves. In a panic, the (4) _____

grabbed a (8) _____ and threw

it at the (6) _____. Luckily, a

(9) _____ arrived to save the day.

The (6) _____ ran away,

never to be seen again.

6

N. is for NOVELTY

Imagine your brain is like the universe. Your personal universe-brain is filled with a wide array of stars made from experiences, memories, relationships, and concepts. Now, imagine that divergent, creative, anything-is-possible thinking as a super-fast spaceship, moving at light speed around the universe collecting ingredients from random stars.

Someone with a wide diversity of experiences, who has sought different points of view, with a diverse social network, will have a massive universe stretching across the sky. Now, their divergent spaceship can go anywhere — *"To infinity and beyond!"*[20] This spaceship will curate ingredients from a wide assortment of stars, leading to more novel insights and breakthrough ideas. Sometimes, the ideas might even be out of this world (pun intended). Maybe you are the only human on Earth has that unique combination of stars

---

20 Thank you, Buzz Lightyear, for this brilliant quote! Find the link under Ch. 6 at thereluctantcreative.com/resources

in their universe-brain. The result is a delicious cornucopia of flavours and fusion cuisine for the soul. Or, more practically speaking, your unique universe brain might provide the lottery-winning insight to solve that un-solvable problem facing your business.

However, someone who stays comfortable, who does the same things over and over, who doesn't take chances or try to stretch their comfort zone? A much smaller universe. Their spaceship travels around a much smaller solar system, collecting homogeneous thoughts and ingredients. Mashed potatoes for dinner, again? This universe is as well travelled as the I-95 or the 401, and unlikely to produce anything unique or interesting.

Additionally, collecting new experiences and trying new things is like the Fountain of Youth for your brain. In David Eagleman's book, *Livewired*, Eagleman explains how we change our brain in every interaction. The act of trying new things, forcing our brain to adapt to writing with the wrong hand, or tackling something in a new way, keeps our brain growing and making new connections. If you don't challenge your brain, it will atrophy and shrink like a wool sweater in the dryer. Dr. Eagleman recounts the story of group of nuns at a convent, where many nuns were diagnosed post-mortem with Alzheimer's. Their Alzheimer's was unapparent when the nuns were alive, because they were constantly challenged to think differently and discuss cerebral topics, learn new skills, and contribute to the group. Use it or lose it.

Seeking novelty expands our universe-brain to allow more connections between concepts. In *Success Hangover*, Kelsey Ramsden calls it "new ingredients." If you want to make vanilla cake every day, then sure, stock the same stuff in your pantry. But, if you want a different kind of cake, or creative ideas, or even a different level of vanilla, you are going to have to go shopping.

YOU CAN SEEK NOVELTY WITH INTENTION.

First, you need to get over the discomfort of trying something different, especially if you have been well within your comfort zone for years. What helped me was to identify my process of resistance, as described in Chapter Two, so I can see it coming and have a plan of attack to defeat it. You can start small. You can download a list to get you started at thereluctantcreative.com/resources.

Ask your newsagent or librarian to recommend a magazine that you would never normally read. Get off the bus a stop early and walk the rest of the way. Buy a new coffee flavour at a local shop, not knowing if you'll like it or not. Meet new friends, including ones from different cultural backgrounds. Go to a cultural festival, eat at an ethnic restaurant. Learn a new language, as bilingualism has been proven to make you more creative.

Travel is another great way to find new creative ingredients. If live travel isn't at your fingertips, try travelling online to new museums, prehistoric Earth, and even a virtual journey through a nebula (look on Google Arts and Culture and other sites promoting virtual tours). If you want to do an Olympics-level exploration, pick up the book *The Wander Society* by Keri Smith, who details a somewhat secret society of wanderers who explore uncertainty and allow life to delight and surprise them at every turn. There is no destination to a good wander, only a curious mind, ample time, and a means of locomotion. Become a Flaneur, as described in Chapter Four — D. is for Daydream. You already have everything you need.

Once upon a time, I experienced novelty on a visit to a friend in New York City. When we visited the Metropolitan Museum of Art, the special exhibit at the time was on *Camp*[21]. *Camp* is the unique, flamboyant style and aesthetic popularized by stars like Cher, Lady Gaga, and Elton John. I knew very little about *Camp*, and I was not particularly interested in fashion. Honestly, nothing about the exhibit description drew me in. But that's exactly why I went. The exhibit was amazing. I was fascinated with the history and evolution of *Camp*. The outfits were out of this world! There was a dress made to look like leftovers on a tray, another dress looked like butterflies fluttering around a shower poof.

---

21 Learn more about Camp under Ch. 6 at thereluctantcreative.com/resources

Yet, I did not turn into a *Camp* fan. I'm not joining *Camp* discussion groups, collecting *Camp* memorabilia, or wearing a meat dress in Lady Gaga style to pick up my kids from school (but that sounds like a fun idea...). But maybe in a year, or five years, or 10 years, something from that exhibit will spark an idea and make a connection to another concept that I'm working on and result in amazing aha or insight. Sadly, I might not even realize that *Camp* was the source for the idea, to give it proper credit.

If you find comfort in the familiar, join the club. In Chapter Five — A. is for Ambiguity, we explored our fascination with certainty. If you prefer a conservative approach, you can still seek new experiences and, as the title of this book claims, effortlessly expand your comfort zone. Maybe you won't choose stand-up comedy, rock climbing, or scuba diving like me. You might start with ordering a different sandwich on the menu, walking to the bathroom a different way, watching a tv show that was not on your wish list, speaking up at a meeting, or taking an online course on surviving a Zombie Apocalypse[22].

Seeking novelty can be uncomfortable, especially if our efforts are public. Discomfort is the price we must pay to stretch our comfort zone and grow. People who are physically fit know this — you can't get six-pack abs by eating ice cream and watching Netflix (although I keep creatively

---

22   True story — you can take a course to survive a Zombie Apocalypse.
Find it under Ch. 6 at thereluctantcreative.com/resources

trying to figure this out!). This discomfort requires us to dig into our process for overcoming resistance.

There are so many ways to avoid discomfort; social media, paper pushing, punching a clock, counting the hours until quitting time, Candy Crush. These are also uncomfortable, but more like the fetid stagnation hiding in a closed garbage bag full of wet grass that has been sitting in the sun (ooh can you smell it?). Choose your discomfort. You can choose the discomfort of growth or the discomfort of stagnation. I repeat this to my kids when I'm asking them to do their chores — choose the discomfort of doing the chore or the discomfort of losing allowance and privileges. They love it (I think) when I impart these helpful tidbits of life wisdom.

Risky Business

I have become pretty good at risk/benefit evaluation and risk mitigation. The proof, I guess, is that I'm still alive and writing this book. The mantra "But will you DIE?" is what helps me get up on stage for comedy, try a difficult rock climbing route, go backcountry camping, or travelling the world solo. Sometimes, there is a possibility I will die. And I could also die while eating a cheezie sitting on the couch. My approach includes a 360° evaluation of the possibilities, daydreaming about multiple storylines in alternate dimensions. For example, when rock climbing, there is a risk I could fall. To mitigate the risk of a calamity, I take safety very seriously. I never miss a partner or rope check and

I only climb with people I trust. *Okay, so what if I do fall?* I'm on a rope, I have checked all the gear, and people climb every day without hurting themselves. *How would I die?* If the safety measures failed or there was a perilous act like a lightning strike that I can't predict. *What are the chances?* Probably not. You get the picture.

For stand-up comedy, it's much easier. I won't die (literally). I might want to crawl up under a rock and disappear, but the risk of personal injury is insignificant. Well, I guess that might depend on the venue, especially if someone is drinking champagne, since champagne corks kill about two dozen people per year,[23] but that gets covered in risk mitigation.

What pushes me through to reach the literal, or figurative summit might be different than what pushes you. Find out what works for you and harness it to pull you to the top. Scribble a few of your own ideas like "But did you die?" for what to tell your inner Todd when he is trying to keep you artificially safe. Cowabunga? Just do it? Don't be chicken? What would motivate you to expand your comfort zone, even a little bit? Discover your own source of courage to taste the entirety of life's buffet. There's more to life than garlic bread. Just be careful with the champagne.

---

23   Random trivia you never thought you'd learn, right? Read more under Chapter 6 at thereluctantcreative.com/resources

Random Ingredient Dare

Go to perchance.org/ingredient or randomlists.com/food and get 1-3 ingredients. Find a recipe using these ingredients.  (Video: Random Ingredient Dare*)

Easy mode: draw the recipe you found.

Hard mode: Make the recipe and write about the experience making it.

_____

_____

_____

_____

_____

_____

Random Reading

Easy mode: Read an article you would usually scroll past. What was your reaction when you first saw it?

▶ (Video: Storycorps Dare*)

_____

_____

_____

_____

_____

_____

_____

_____

_____

_____

_____

See next page for Hard Mode

* Find the video and a PDF download of this sheet at thereluctantcreative.com/resources

Hard mode: Read a random book.

▶ **(Video: Library Magazine Dare*)**

Here are some ideas of how to choose one:

- Pick a number from 1 to 1000 and read a book with that dewey decimal number from the library

- Swap a random book with a friend and commit to reading it

- Use a free little library in your neighborhood

- Type your initials into Kindle or Kobo and choose the 10th book in the list to read

Jot down your thoughts. (Take note that a strong positive or negative reaction can indicate unconscious bias.)

_____

_____

_____

_____

_____

_____

_____

_____

_____

_____

_____

7

C. is for CURIOSITY

When Sir. Alexander Fleming came back from spring break[24] with a hangover and a tan, he was horrified to come back to a dirty lab. In his rush to pack his Speedo for his trip to Spain, he had left his microbiology supplies in disarray. Disgusted, he cleaned up the mess[25] by dumping the petri dishes into a sterilizing solution.

He paused when he noticed something weird. He got curious.

He looked carefully at the petri dish he held in his hands, full of mold and bacteria. A clear ring surrounded one of the tufts of mold, like an invisible barrier between the mold and the bacteria. Many years later, that mold

---

24 I may have taken a few liberties with the story of Penicillin, I hope you don't mind.

25 It's no coincidence that Dr. Alex had to clean up his own lab instead of getting a female housekeeper to do it—another good reason why gender roles are a bad idea and why men should clean up after themselves. If he didn't clean up his own mess maybe we wouldn't have antibiotics today. That's the story I'm telling my boys anyway. They love it (I think) when I share these words of wisdom as they are scrubbing the toilets.

developed into the life-saving drug we know as Penicillin, but it started with curiosity.

An Academic Horror Show

People are the most curious when they know a little bit about something and are highly driven for the answer. Experts and mouth-breathing troglodytes have low curiosity. Sometimes it's hard to tell the difference. Such is the argument for the Dunning-Krueger effect: you can be so stupid that you don't even know you're stupid. The Dunning-Kruger effect is widely touted to explain (often political) behaviour. Smug academics nod in agreement and angst for all the (other) stupid people in the world. In an interesting twist, there have been new questions about the relevance and validity of the original work cited in the Dunning-Kruger effect.

But, for argument's sake, if you were quite stupid but did not know it, you would be very confident in your (lack of) knowledge, therefore less curious. Thus, continues the vicious cycle of ignorance.

Where would we be without curiosity? And what has happened to our curiosity? Thanks to the Internet, we can find a "credible" source that passionately espouses whatever we think is right. Ubiquitous confirmation bias. People on both sides of a charged issue are 1000% confident in the validity of their point of view. Add social media's frenetic drive to show you only the things that you agree with, "cancel culture," and an addiction to outrage, it's no wonder why people are polarized. If you foster a mindset of intellectual humility, the wisdom to know that you don't have all the answers, at home and at work, you will make better decisions, be easier to work with, and have a more open mindset for creativity. Gone are the days of unequivocally following an expert's advice, as evidenced by the anti-vaccine movement, many armchair "experts" from the school of "I Googled it," and my kids' refusal to eat their vegetables. I have seen an evolution in my own veterinary practice of over 20 years. As a new graduate, people would ask, "Doc, what should I do?" It was a short-ish conversation. I told them what I thought was going on, what tests I needed to do and the cost, and how serious I thought it was. Then I would say something like, "Well, Mr. Smith, you have three options. The gold standard option is the most expensive, but we are most likely to get a diagnosis and the best treatment. Then there is the silver, where we might cut a few diagnostic or treatment corners, but the bulk of the needed items are there. Then there's the bronze. We can try a few things, we probably won't find out the cause, and we might get lucky. Or we might not. Here are the costs for each."

More recently, since the invention of daily Internet use, really, my conversations with pet owners have lengthened to 45-minute discussions with all family members about all the stories that I might create to explain the symptoms in the pet. People have always wanted a dollar store medical magic wand, but now they want a full medical degree crash course condensed into a 20-minute appointment. The bulk of my time is spent addressing misinformation — what the breeder, the pet store owner, the neighbour, or the random person on the subway knows about a topic. These conversations are exhausting, because it takes a great deal of cognitive effort to keep a straight face when you smell BS (and I've smelt a lot of it).

That said, I actually love the Internet for my pet parents, because it makes my life so much easier...if or when the information is valid. And some of the internet suggestions are worth investigating, which is when my intellectual humility is important. But let's get real here, people do the weirdest things to their pets sometimes. For the record, NONE of the following remedies have worked, despite the optimism of their "care" takers: Greek yoghurt in an ear to cure a yeast infection, coconut oil for fleas, beer baths for itchy dogs, and, from my large animal associates, an onion in a horse's rectum for colic.

Leaders on a Perilous Pedestal

Leaders are expected to have all the answers, so their confidence is what's admired and promoted.

Unfortunately, vulnerability and curiosity are often perceived as negative leadership traits. However, studies show that more effective leaders and scientists have intellectual humility — the wisdom to know that they don't have all the answers. It's easy to mistake bravado and confidence for competence. We tend to see things as they are, not as they should be, which explains our attachment to confidently useless leaders. Can you think of one? Jot their name in the margin. Feel free to add some curse words, emojis and inappropriate squiggles. Go for it!

In Dr. Jennifer Mueller's book, *Creative Change: Why We Resist It...How We Can Embrace It,* she explains that we tend to promote leaders who look like existing leaders, not because they are effective, but because we have created an image of what a leader "should" look like, even if they stink. We need to change the narrative around leadership. We have the ability, with awareness, to change the narrative with our votes, and support leaders who show more effective qualities. Everyone is a leader or expert either within a team, our family, or as leaders of our own lives.

Curious Experts, Chihuahuas, and Concerned Cats

It's hard to be curious and have intellectual humility, especially when you are supposed to be the expert in the room. A veterinarian clearly did not utter the adage "curiosity killed the cat." Curiosity did not kill the cat. Obesity, bad luck, electrical cords, lily poisoning, inadequate veterinary care, yes. Curiosity, a hard no.

Curiosity did, however, save the life of one of my patients. I was working at a clinic in Florida, shortly after graduation, on a busy Saturday. A client—we called him Mr. Assuming—phoned to ask for the dose of Benadryl for one of his two Chihuahuas, Thumper (Joey was the other pup). Sue, the technologist (nurse) had answered the phone, and she stopped me as I rushed to my next appointment. "Mr. Assuming called. He says Thumper was stung by a bee in the yard and needs a dose of Benadryl."

Distracted, I grabbed a calculator. "How much does Thumper weigh?"

"Eight pounds," Sue replied.

I typed the numbers into the calculator when something triggered my curiosity. I asked Sue why Mr. Assuming thought Thumper had been stung by a bee. Sue leveled me with the well-known phenomenon of technologist-to-new-graduate-rolling-stink-eye, and said, "I don't know, you can talk to him if you want." I was already running late; I didn't have time for this, but curiosity—and my intellectual humility—got the better of me.

"Hi Mr. Assuming. Sue tells me Thumper was stung by a bee?"

"Yes, earlier this morning."

"Did you see what happened?"

"No. But it must have been a bee because he seemed fine before he went outside."

"What did you notice?"

"He doesn't seem to want to move, and he is very depressed."

"Is there a lump anywhere?"

"No, but he is very sore."

"I think we should take a quick look, to be sure."

We took a "quick" look at Thumper, who, in the end, had not been stung by a bee. Thumper had eaten mouse poison, which interferes with his blood's ability to clot. Mouse poisoned animals bleed spontaneously, anywhere. Brain, heart, abdomen, and in Thumper's case, his joints. Mr. Assuming had made an uneducated guess. In this case, it was wrong, and we luckily caught it in time and were able to administer the medications and care that Thumper needed. Thumper pulled through.

What amazed me the most was that we had just completed the same treatment for Mr. Assuming's other dog, Joey, who had also eaten some mouse poison weeks before. I gave Mr. Assuming the diagnosis, and he replied "well, I saw him carrying some around in his mouth, but I didn't think he ate any." Yes, I made that face too. I had not yet mastered the ninja skill of exercising my will over my poker facial expressions.

Now, before you conclude that Mr. Assuming is an idiot, his actions make sense given what we know about curiosity. He landed in the "I don't know anything about it" area of the curiosity curve. Conversely, I know how to treat a bee sting, so I was on the expert end of the curiosity curve. Thumper's case humbled me in a way I have never forgotten. Thumper was a calculator entry away from death. Thumper is my North Star for intellectual humility, compelling me to sit in the discomfort of ambiguity and to get curious. If you are annoyed at your tardy veterinarian, or at the seemingly "unnecessary" tests they recommend, I hope you also consider Thumper's story.

What is Curiosity . . . Diversive or Specific?

Not all curiosity is the same. There are a few different ways to look at curiosity, one of which is driven by the source of motivation. It's the difference between "I just HAVE to know the answer" and "I wonder what it could be...?"

Someone probably jumps to mind when you consider each type. When I'm reading an amazing novel, I'm driven to know the answer. Sometimes I'm tempted to skip to the end just to resolve the pain of not knowing whodunnit (I know...ambiguity. I'm practicing). But here, I'm driven by specific curiosity. Conversely, when I am problem solving a dilemma with a friend, I default to "what if" thinking, or diversive curiosity. When my friends come to me for advice, they expect a long discussion and evaluation of all possibilities and the pros and cons of each. They love it (I think) when we spend hours exploring all the creative ways they might get their own kids to eat vegetables.

These two main types of curiosity are:

1. **Diversive Curiosity** — the interest to learn something new, explore the unfamiliar. People with high diversive curiosity seek out novelty for feelings of excitement. They seek a broad variety of information instead of a specific solution. They are curious because they just want to know *why*? *What else* could there be?

2. **Specific Curiosity** — the desire to reduce uncertainty and resolve a knowledge gap. Specific curiosity is problem focused and dedicated to decreasing novelty in the environment. They are curious because they can't stand not knowing *the* answer.

In Chapter Five — A. is for Ambiguity, we talked about having a high Tolerance of Ambiguity (TOA) as being a positive trait for success. Someone with a very low TOA can have specific curiosity, driven by a desire for certainty, not for possibility. Mr. Assuming needed to resolve the ambiguity about the cause for Thumper's symptoms. With his limited medical knowledge, he might have put the known pieces together to resolve the knowledge gap, then decided that Thumper was stung by a bee.

Kids, on the other hand, provide great examples of diversive curiosity. In one study, a teacher showed a new toy to preschool children. One group was shown the toy and given instructions on how it worked. The other group was given the toy and allowed to explore. The group with the teacher's explanation lost interest in the toy sooner and did not find other features of the toy on their own. The diverse curiosity soared among the kids without the explanation, because they knew a little about the toy and had high motivation for discovering all the cool features of the toy. They had no preconceived notions about how it worked.

To Mr. Assuming, believing that Thumper was stung by a bee reduced his anxiety, because now he thought he knew what to do. But it, unfortunately, was wrong. What if Mr. Assuming had called this "intuition?" He "just knew" that Thumper had been stung by a bee. People say to "trust your intuition" but sometimes I just think that's giving people permission to accept unconscious bias and flawed logic, and to avoid curiosity. What was great about Mr. Assuming was that he was open to being curious, he exercised intellectual humility by bringing Thumper in for an examination, and he accepted THE solution when it was clear the initial thought wasn't right.

Not surprisingly, curiosity positively predicts creative performance. Some have considered diversive curiosity to be unproductive and unfocused, like a bored teenager flipping channels, while touting specific curiosity as the holy grail of discovery — like a scientist finding an answer to life's mysteries. Recent studies have placed more focus on diversive curiosity, especially in early stages, and when the problem is ambiguous or complex.

Specific curiosity can still help creativity. In a series of experiments involving participants making guesses about how Houdini made an elephant disappear, researchers found that specific curiosity helps creativity through a concept called "idea linking." Brainstorming with divergent thinking works by disconnecting from previous ideas, to try to diverge away from what we already know. Idea linking works by building on early ideas, which become indispensable to the next idea, and so on, in a sequential manner. According to researchers, idea linking is not an automatic process in creative tasks. Idea linking can harness the drive from being frustrated about "wanting to know" into creative solutions. So, like anything in life, curiosity is complicated.

Specific curiosity — and annoyance at burrs in his dog's coat — compelled George de Mestral, a Swiss engineer, to discover the hook and loop explanation for how the burr stuck to his dog. However, it was diversive curiosity that fueled the market for Velcro and applications for everyday use.

"BE LESS CURIOUS ABOUT PEOPLE AND MORE CURIOUS ABOUT IDEAS."

— Marie Curie

Corporate Curiosity

Companies say they want curious employees because of the association of curiosity with engagement, creativity, and innovation. But are they willing to pay the price? Curiosity also requires autonomy, responsibility, and freedom according to the Merck State of Curiosity Report[26]. It seems simple, so why are so many organizations falling short?

Despite the fanfare about curiosity, 65% of respondents report barriers to curiosity. Barriers include:

- Top-down work

- Lack of exchange with other teams, and

- Constant surveillance.

Interestingly, 90% of employees who self-report as curious say that they have support for curiosity at work.

Merck has proved that curiosity can be increased and taught in teams. Through their ACTIVATE Curiosity program, diverse teams were given an innovation goal with targeted recommendations, technical guidance, and video tutorials for six months. Participants were satisfied with the program, became more curious, and made important progress on or even completed their goals. What was unanticipated were benefits which included

- Open communication

- Teamwork and collaboration

---

26 Find the link to the whole report under Ch. 7 at thereluctantcreative.com/resources

- Active participation and engagement, and

- Fresh perspectives.

In other research, a curious workplace has fewer decision-making errors, more innovation, less group conflict, and better team performance (through communication).

Maybe you can't teach an old dog new tricks, but you can teach him how to discover brand new ones.

Additionally, Merck linked curiosity to innovation, which should not really be a shock to anyone, but proof is always nice. Merck concluded that a one-point increase in curiosity correlates to a 0.68 increase in innovation within an organization[27].

Curiosity's Creative Evolution

Curiosity research is evolving rapidly, but it's a challenge. What is the definition, and how is it measured, if it can be? Curiosity is associated with creativity, but the mechanism is slowly coming into focus. Steve Jobs and Walt Disney have credited curiosity for their creative output. Curiosity predicts positive job performance and rapid adaptation in organizations. With our tsunami of change hitting the workplace in the next five to ten years, 50% or more of employees are predicted to require a job change or significant reskilling. Dr. Diane Hamilton calls curiosity "one of the most critical determinants of performance." It's

---

27 Curious about your curiosity? You can find the self test under Ch. 7 at thereluctantcreative.com/resources

clear that curiosity is a key driver for organizational success, as well as a personal motivator for individuals to seek new challenges, learn new skills, and keep pace with future job requirements. *Curiosity positively correlates with intellectual humility. TOA, and creativity.* Intellectual humility is driven by truth-seeking, not by a narcissistic need to be right, which I think would be a refreshing change if nothing else. *Curiosity is a foundational pillar of creativity.* Uncertainty in response to ambiguity interferes with our ability to be curious. If you remember from Chapter Five — A. is for Ambiguity, not knowing has been proven to create a threat-like response, which sends us into information seeking mode, and pushes us to finding a solution — usually one that has worked in the past. We can change our reactions if we build awareness and get curious about our response to ambiguity. Research is now revealing that if we can sit comfortably in an ambivalent state, and accept ambiguity with more equanimity, we will increase our creative potential. Ultimately, all kinds of curiosity drive creative solutions.

Engaging curiosity is the first step in admitting to yourself that you know a little bit, but not everything about a topic. Use intellectual humility to collect information through diverse curiosity, then use your divergent creativity to consider many possibilities. Finally, narrow down to a workable solution using convergent creativity and specific curiosity.

Curiosity also puts you at a huge advantage in the workplace. People who are curious are more likely to enter a flow state that Adam Grant describes as instrumental to happiness during the pandemic, and also leads to creative solutions from happier employees.

Curiosity in the Workplace

Check the benefits noticed by curious employees in Germany and the US. (See the bottom of this page for answers.)

☐ Higher job satisfaction

☐ Cat owners

☐ Job crafting

☐ Star Wars fans

☐ Innovation

☐ Read fiction

☐ Work engagement

☐ Afraid of heights

☐ Healthy work relationships

☐ No notifications on phone

Answers: Higher job satisfaction, Work engagement, Job crafting, Healthy work relationships

Curiosity can improve mental well-being. Paired like a fine wine with Creativity brie and TOA crackers, it increases our mood and resilience.

And finally, being curious makes life way more fun. Which is important because curious people also live longer.

Awe and Curiosity

Have you ever been drawn into an experience that completely consumed your attention and time seemed to stand still? I recall this effect in a recent moment in time when my son noticed the weather outside. We gazed out of the window, watching the shapeshifting clouds create a dramatic display in a brewing thunderstorm. We talked about where the clouds might be headed, watched the lightning streak across the sky, and marveled at the frenetic dance of nature. I found myself in awe of the magnificence of nature. I wasn't thinking about anything else. I was fully present and immersed in the experience of watching the power of nature, and the magical connection with my son.

We engaged our curiosity, found magic in the storm, and through mindfulness we discovered awe. You can do it right now. Stop for a second and feel the page (or the plastic e-reader case) of this book.

I SAID, STOP FOR A SECOND
AND FEEL THE PAGE

(OR THE E-READER CASE,
OR YOUR KEYBOARD).

How did we go from living in caves to manufacturing a mechanism to capture our stories in print? Can you imagine? Take that tree in your backyard or park and...turn it into paper? Isn't it amazing that a tree can grow and produce material for humanity to capture art, science, knowledge, and more? Consider this page. The molecules inside the page, the ink, and the process to print the book are truly incredible. If you can get curious about what seems routine and banal, you can experience awe every day.

Awe makes us feel small, yet deeply connected to the world, according to neuroscientist Dr. Beau Lotto from the Lab of Misfits. Dr. Lotto ties together the connection between awe and curiosity in his unique and entertaining (and awesome) TED Talk, complete with artists and Cirque du Soleil performances[28].

Go ahead watch it. It's that good. I'll wait. Scribble some notes in the margin right here.

Welcome back! We're not yet done with awe and curiosity.

Awe increases our prosocial behaviour and inspires us to step into uncertainty. It's easy to feel in awe, if you use curiosity to engage fully in the present moment.

Where can you find awe today? In the smile of your child, the flexibility of your cat, the light reflecting off the bird bath, or even the mystery of the Caramilk Bar[29]. What would you be willing to pay for bringing awe into your life?

---

28 Find the link to Dr. Beau Lott's TED Talk under Ch. 7 at thereluctantcreative.com/resources
29 Watching these ads from the '80s might even spur awe around how far we have come with special effects and picture resolution...AND give you the secret to the Caramilk! Find the link under Ch. 7 at thereluctantcreative.com/resources

Curiosity Dare

What was the last thing you ate? Google how it's made and the nutritional facts. Write some interesting facts here.

📽️ (Video: Curious About Food Dare*)

Interesting Fact #1

_____

_____

Interesting Fact #2

_____

_____

Interesting Fact #3

_____

_____

Interesting Fact #4

_____

_____

Interesting Fact #5

_____

_____

Guildfords Alternate Uses Test

Find something you can see right now. What other things could you use it for? Write anything that comes to mind even if it sounds silly.

_____

_____

_____

_____

_____

_____

_____

_____

_____

_____

What if you had 1000 of them?

_____

_____

_____

_____

8

E. is for EDIT LATER

Dr. George Land (our NASA kindergarten quiz friend) compares our divergent, imaginative thinking to the gas pedal, and our convergent, editing, critical thinking to the brake. Both types of creativity are important. Most people try unsuccessfully to do both at the same time. Imagine you just robbed a bank. You jump into the getaway car, and put the gas pedal to the metal, to get the heck out of there. Then (for reasons unknown), you slam on the brake at the same time. Can't imagine? I'll try to explain, from the perspective of a K-Mart parking lot.

K-Mart was a fun place to work in high school. Looking back, one of the greatest things about the job was the diversity among the teenage employees. Metalheads, bookworms, drama hippies, geeks, we all worked together and had fun.

My family had two cars at that point with two driving teenagers in the house: a Datsun and (inexplicably) a

Camaro Z28. I was embarrassed to drive the Camaro — it seemed too flashy. Give me a break, I was a teenager, I was embarrassed about everything.

One evening, two of the guys I worked with, Dan and Jeff, convinced me to let them drive the Camaro. We headed out to the parking lot, which was completely empty — the mall was closed, and everyone had gone home. Dan got in the driver's side, I was in the passenger side, and Jeff was sulking in the cramped backseat.

Dan drove the car around the parking lot a few times, and then put the car in neutral and smiled across at Jeff and me and exclaimed "Brake Stand!" Suddenly, he slammed his foot on the accelerator and brake at the same time.[30] A high pitched, deafening noise, the strong smell of burning rubber and the thrum of the car underneath me overwhelmed my senses. I could feel the power of the car, but I looked out the window to see that we weren't going anywhere. Except maybe to jail, or at least to an early curfew from now on.

How many times have you been sitting in a meeting with a great idea, but you don't speak up because you thought your unique idea might be stupid? Or you worry that the other people might think the idea was stupid? Or you discover a new way to do something but avoid trying it out because nobody else does it that way, so it must be wrong…sort of like how I felt in the passenger seat of that

---

30 For a brake stand (or burnout) video find the link under Ch. 8 at thereluctantcreative.com/resources

Camaro only the smoke is coming from your ears instead of the tires.

This brings us to our last strategy in **D.A.N.C.E.** — E for Edit Later. This is one of the seemingly easiest, yet most important concepts to apply to your creativity. Great thinkers like Hemmingway used this strategy when he said, "Write drunk, edit sober," and Picasso bemoaned "The greatest enemy to creativity is good sense." Many writers, creativity advocates, and kindergarteners recognize the benefits of just doing the "shitty first draft," the first sketch, or the first mud pie without trying to think about whether it's "good," or "woke," or "round enough."

No Bad Ideas

Now, don't get me wrong, there are some bad solutions. Some really, truly, very bad solutions. But ideas are neutral. There is a time to evaluate ideas, just not in the idea generation phase. Challenging ideas does lead to better solutions, but it's best to wait until the ideas are expressed first. You don't have to be drunk to create better ideas, which actually decreases creativity (sorry Ernest) because you don't have the brain function to be able to capture and do something with your ideas. But you do have to loosen your inhibitions, turn off your critic, and suspend judgement. Kids are great at this because they are (I'll say it again) clueless. They also don't have a well-heeled cynical critic yet to tell them what is impossible, nor a massive rejection filter to consider how their ideas might change others' perceptions of them.

You might envy a colleague or celebrity who just doesn't seem to give a flying duck (thank you, autocorrect) about what others think of them. How did they get there? Practice. They certainly did not get that Oscar or Grammy by making safe choices with no mistakes.

Once you start sharing your ideas without editing them first, you realize that nobody really thinks about you that much anyway. Also, if you play it safe, to avoid criticism and rejection, you will likely remain in the comfy pit of complacency and mediocrity. And the trolls, the haters, the critics? Everything in life is like a bell curve. Some people are going to hate you or your ideas, then some will love you or your ideas, and most people are somewhere in the middle. If I'm lucky enough to get some book reviews for this book, I would almost bet the farm that there will be a few people who will hate it (please don't hate it though). So, when you use your big brain to override your survival mechanism (remember that inner Todd) and share your creative gifts with the world, you expect the criticism. As my mother always says, "you can't please everyone!" Use statistics to explain the criticism — a statistically significant and expected part of the bell curve of making a difference. Judgement is simply a mathematical inevitability, my friend. And if the feedback is cruel, personal, unhelpful, and inflammatory? Don't let them succeed in pulling you back inside the bucket of crabs[31]. The threat of someone speaking their mind and

---

31   Did you know that crabs pull each other down? Now you do. Find the explanation under Ch. 8 at thereluctantcreative.com/resources

sharing their creative self gives some people such anxiety that they can't stand it. Like crabs in a bucket, if you try to climb out there is always a crab that pulls you back in, because your escape is too uncomfortable for them.

You have a brain, a creative one to boot — so use it. We are all victims of our unconscious patterns of behaviour, but the great thing about having that giant frontal cortex is that we can start to be aware of how we edit our own ideas. Then, we can start to change our reaction, a bit at a time, and slowly expand our comfort zone for sharing our message.

Here are a few practical ways to start editing later so you do not stop your — or anyone else's — ideas from flowing without judgement.

1. **Keep a notebook close** by or use the dictation setting on your phone (Siri, Google, otter, etc.). Many people find that great ideas come to them while they are doing something else — driving a car, having a shower, etc. If you think about them too much, you might edit them down to a more lukewarm and less novel version. Write (or record) ideas down as soon as you get them. Stand-up comics use this technique — if you've ever seen a comedian off the stage, you will probably notice they have a notebook or app that they use to jot down interesting observations.

2. **Better brainstorming.** Allow everyone to independently write down their ideas in the idea generation

phase, instead of telling the sentry at the white board. Alternate between individual work and group discussion. Adding or removing constraints to the problem often makes room for new ideas. For a product, think of adding or removing essential features, narrowing the target market, or using specific materials. When I take groups through the Creative Education Foundation's Creative Problem Solving framework, we use a variety of excellent (and fun — always fun) tools to enable efficient divergent and convergent thinking[32].

3. **Practice noticing your inner critic** and tell them to take a short hike. You'll need them later. You too can call them Todd if you like or choose another name that resonates.

4. **Practice rejection.** You could do what I do and perform stand-up comedy, a sure recipe for developing a thick skin. Or start a bit smaller, like sharing some ideas with colleagues, or trying a new spot for coffee, or using a new font on a memo. Get comfortable with the possibility of rejection and failure to teach your body that it's not going to die. That YOU'RE not going to die. Not on my watch, Todd! ☺ Train yourself to accept rejection as the price you need to pay to get to the great ideas. The more you do it, the less it stings. I promise. You'll also realize that your

---

32 Find out more about Creative Problem Solving at the link under Ch. 8 at thereluctantcreative.com/resources

confidence to face uncertainty gives others permission to do the same. Other ideas include improvisation classes, any kind of class really, speaking groups such as Toastmasters, ventriloquism, learn an instrument, join a choir, make a Hallowe'en costume, try curling, go birdwatching, sign up (and then go to) a dance class, the sky's the limit, including skydiving!

5. **Ditch the assumptions. Be a clueless kindergart-
    ener.** Again, kids are cluelessly assumption-less. To become more divergent in your thinking you must engage with a beginner's mind; remember "Shoshin." Peter Skillman developed a collaborative problem solving exercise. Here, he had two different groups — one a team of business school students, the other... kindergartners. He asked these two groups to build the highest tower out of 20 pieces of spaghetti, one yard of tape, one yard of string and a single marsh-mallow that must be on the top. The team that didn't succeed? Business Students. The team that did? Kindergarteners. Why was this? None of the kids tried to became CEOs or jockey for power. The business students spent a lot of time in status nego-tiation. Whereas the kindergarteners jumped in and started iterating, not worrying much about "getting it right." Since this collaborative experiment, many team building facilitators and consultants use this exercise in corporate workshops.

ARE YOU NOTICING THAT THERE'S A THEME? WE REALLY DID LEARN ALL WE EVER NEEDED TO BY THE TIME WE WERE IN **KINDERGARTEN!**

Try the Freefall Writing Technique

Set a timer for a few minutes and write without stopping. If you can't think of the next word, keep your hand moving—draw swirls or lines while you think. Here is a prompt to start: **"The forest was quiet..."**

You can use this technique over and over again!

Finish the Drawing

9

Will You D.A.N.C.E. With Me?

f you started reading this book as a reluctant creative, you might still resist the idea of engaging your inner, elemental personal gift. Perhaps you're a bit like me — it's easier to read a book than put it into practice. I read (and forget) a lot of books. I'm addicted to learning, it's a problem. It's easier to "know" something than do it. Reading a book is safe — nobody has to even know what you are reading about. Safety is an illusion and with the massive changes in progress at work, you had better start taking some chances to learn how to swim before your water wings pop. In the future of work, if you want to feel more satisfied at work, more connected to your purpose, your unique contribution in this world, start by engaging your creativity in only a few minutes a day. It is uncomfortable to change how we show up in the world. The inner critics, your own "Todds" of the world, try to keep us safe in the best way they know how — and it has worked for thousands of years. It won't work anymore, so it's time to engage our human frontal cortex and take Todd by the hand and into the future. You can even feed him vegetables.

Start Now

My friend Lori is an accomplished stand-up comedian. Like most performers during the COVID pandemic, her gigs were cancelled. To help pass the time, Lori found inspiration in art. She had never painted before, but inspiration struck in the form of a box of old nail polish. She describes how the box spoke to her and said, "Make something with me." She searched online and found a technique called "hydropaint." She filled a tub with water, then dripped and swirled the nail polish on the water to create patterns. Once Lori dipped her canvas into the pattern, voila! A beautiful and abstract work of art. I remember seeing Lori's early works posted on Facebook. By engaging and sharing with her own creativity, she inspired it in others. Friends and strangers loved to comment on what they could "see" in her painting. A polar bear, a fairy, a field full of flowers. One year after her first attempt, she had sold over 100 paintings, which helped to supplement her lost income from performance during the pandemic. I watched the progression of her art and skill. At first, the images were very random. One of her first paintings turned out like a lady's face.

Now, Lori plans her works with a bit more intention. Recently, a fan commissioned a piece from Lori, but wanted specific colours. In her mind, she planned out the sequence of colours, the background, the accent colours. She initially struggled because she couldn't picture a finished piece of art with that colour combination. These were constraints to her creativity, which can often amplify the final result. Once she moved through the initial struggle, she made some small test canvases, and sent them to a trusted friend who gave some suggestions. Lori tried them and penguins started to appear in her art. The final product was an abstract piece reminiscent of an arctic landscape with a penguin colony (see picture above). Staying open to possibilities propelled her art into an area she could not have predicted. Lori works with both her intuition and outside input to guide her work. When Lori just feels like playing around with her art, with little intention or a plan, she finds that's when she often produces the best result. "Sometimes I just do it when I'm bored, and I don't really plan it out. I'll go grab a few colours and just play with them. Then I'll post it and often it will sell!" Find Lori on instagram @thereal_lorifergusonford.

Lori defines creativity as "When you get inside your own head, you don't let anyone else get in there and just go with it."

You could take Lori's idea and get curious about your own creativity. But, if hydropainting is not your thing, you can still reap many benefits of engaging with your everyday creativity. Start with one minute a day. Instead of taking that minute to feel paralyzed with what to do, remember to **D.A.N.C.E.**

Maybe you're like 25% of Americans who don't engage their creativity. More likely, you are like 75% of Americans who participate in creative activities like gardening, home décor, and cooking everyday meals, but have never considered that "creative" because it didn't seem artistic enough. Half of the people who said they don't do anything creative actually want to do something, they just don't know how to start. Here's the answer.

D.A.N.C.E.

Don't think too much about it, channel your inner kindergartener and start building your creative tower on the fly. You can even dance because it is a very creative outlet. Or simply use the acronym to remember five effortless habits to help your creativity thrive.

A Short D.A.N.C.E. Tutorial

Download the tutorial under Ch. 9 at thereluctantcreative.com/resources

Daydream   Think of an interesting problem or create a foundation for a fantastical story and set a timer for two minutes. Stare out the window and allow whatever thoughts to come without judgement. If you don't have a window, find a photo of nature. Avoid using your phone or desktop because of notifications and distractions. Don't ruminate, inspirate. I know that's not a word. But you know what I mean.

Ambiguity   Take a wrong turn on purpose. Don't plan your meal, just figure it out with the ingredients in your fridge. Ask a server to pick out a coffee, dessert, or even entrée for you. Start practicing ambiguity with small steps and little risk. Remember "But will you DIE?"

Novelty   Go to the Random Word Generator[33] and get a word. Put the word into YouTube and watch the first video that comes up in the search. Or, even better, pull two random words and do the same thing.

---

33 Find the link to a Random Word Generator under Ch. 9 at thereluctantcreative.com/resources

Curiosity When you are waiting for Zoom to connect, or you're put on hold, look at all the things in your environment. Find something that you would otherwise ignore. Ask yourself questions about the origin, function, and development. It could be an item, or a person in a photo, or even a smell. Just dig into your curiosity.

Edit Later Practice building your thick skin and write a poem, sing a song, or share something you made with friends or colleagues in person or on social media. Extra points if it totally sucks. Post with the hashtag #reluctantcreative so we can celebrate our failures together. There is liberation in failing publicly on purpose.

Practice Your D.A.N.C.E.

Some people say you should schedule these things, but that doesn't work for me. Do what works for you. Personally, I resist schedules, so I like to pair it with a physical context.

For example, when I sit down to drink my tea in the morning or afternoon, I sit so that I can look out the window and gaze at the birds on our backyard feeder. Tea is a cue for me to **Daydream**. Maybe an alarm in your calendar works better for you to stop for two minutes and **D.A.N.C.E.**

To engage my ability to tolerate **Ambiguity**, I consciously resist the urge to pick up the smartphone at dinnertime to Google the answer to, "what happened to the actor in the movie you watched?" When I head out for an evening walk or drive to the store, I often randomly turn the opposite way from my natural route. It's my neighbourhood, I know I'm not going to get lost. When completing something with instructions, I jump right in, even if I don't understand the "right" way to do it. This could just be my ADHD, and it drives my husband up the wall. Well, except for setting up a rock climbing rope, or fixing the brakes on your car. Follow those instructions to a tee, please. Avoid peril!

Novelty can be as easy as wearing a new colour, choosing a new music playlist, trying a new online game, or listening to a random podcast. Or, it can be as hard as learning mountaineering, a new language, or how to play Mario Kart Rainbow Road without falling to your death (I'm still practicing this one).

In Dr. David Eagleman's book, *Livewired*, he talks about the importance of new experiences for neuroplasticity. To keep your mind sharp and working optimally, we need to challenge it a little bit every day. And if we challenge our experiences, we can grow new connections, build new habits, and stay sharp well into old age, like the nuns who were surprisingly diagnosed with Alzheimer's after death. For more ambiguity check out the Spotify playlist that I created just for you under Ch. 9 at thereluctantcreative.com/resources.

Curiosity can be woven into every moment of the day. I'm prompted to be curious when I have a strong positive or negative reaction to something — an article, graffiti, a beautiful flower, leftover vegetables on a plate. Strong positive or negative reactions can highlight an unconscious bias. Ask yourself about things you have always taken for granted. Most recently I used curiosity to evaluate my reaction to my son's desire to spend money on fake things in video games. Ugh! Really? But would I rather he purchase plastic crap that is bad for the environment? What is my relationship with value attribution and why do I feel like this is a waste of money? Is it because he plays "too much" video games? Or is there no value because the game is already free? By integrating curiosity with mindfulness, we can precipitate the feeling of awe — a feeling that prompts prosocial behaviour and gives us the confidence to step into uncertainty. There is awe in wall-to-wall carpet, a baby's laugh, a cat's tongue, or a dandelion seed. Channel your inner toddler and ask "why?" My teenagers love it (I think) when I turn these tables on them.

Edit Later. Mindfully construct a space and mindset for editing. Clearly delineate the time to diverge (brainstorm, ideate) then converge (edit and select) at a different time. Never do them together. Remember — no sudden brake stands in your brain!

You can start the principle of **Edit Later** by writing the first thing that comes to mind for a single email or text a day. Write exactly what comes to mind with no edits. Pay attention to your critical inner voice, such as "Todd," who tells you, "They'll think you are weird," or "Sound more professional." Don't send this initial, unedited thought yet! Wait a few hours or a day and then go back and edit the email. Let that hidden voice sing once a day, just for fun. You might be surprised. But still edit the email later. Or send it as is and notice how it feels to be authentically you. Just do you and don't worry so much about the consequences. Don't forget your creativity risk assessment. The people who take bold choices are the ones who change the world, and the ones who get noticed.

Download a list of things you can do to **D.A.N.C.E.** into your regret-proof future in less than a minute at thereluctantcreative.com/resources[34]. Tick off the ones you've done and repeat the ones you hate (and the ones you love).

Starting something new is hard. To engage simple everyday creativity compels you to step into uncertainty and face failure. If this is new for you, it might feel difficult. Cut yourself some slack and be kind to yourself. This is a marathon, not a sprint. For me, two mantras that have helped are "what's the worst that can happen," or "But will you DIE?" always in Ken Jeung's voice from the movie he truly shone in, *The Hangover*.

…Sorry, I got distracted there by a really interesting interview with Ken Jeong about his transition from his career as a medical doctor to actor. Isn't that fascinating? How did

---

34 Download your D.A.N.C.E. list here: thereluctantcreative.com/resources

he get the courage to pursue a creative career? How did he make the transition without going broke? Doesn't that make you curious[35]?

Back to everyday creativity. I recommend that you follow small curiosities for 15-minutes a day. Tell your boss you're working on innovation. It's true. Tell her I told you it was ok.

If judgement from others is holding you back, consider the end of your life. Remember Bronnie Ware from Chapter Two who spent last moments with thousands of people? The top regret was,

"I WISH I'D HAD THE COURAGE TO LIVE A LIFE TRUE TO MYSELF, NOT THE LIFE OTHERS EXPECTED OF ME."

I do not wish this for you.

I hope, dear reader, that you take five minutes every day, to practice these five effortless habits to **D.A.N.C.E.** with your inner creativity and to effortlessly expand your comfort zone. If you want to add some academic rigor (the answer to this question is always YES), you can take a new creativity test, the Divergent Association Task test[36]. Take

---

35 Curious to hear Ken Jeong's interesting story of blending art and science? Check it out under Ch. 9 at thereluctantcreative.com/resources
36 Find a link to the Divergent Association Task Test under Ch. 9 at thereluctantcreative.com/resources

it before you start the strategies, and then every few weeks. I would love to know the results — send me a message at **hello@carolinebrookfield.com** or find me on instagram **@artfulscience** or on Linkedin, or send me a carrier pigeon (PLEASE send me a carrier pigeon!).

Just remember that, like life, your creative exploration is not a linear or isolated process. Use **Curiosity** to ask yourself why you aren't sharing that great idea. Sit in the **Ambiguity** of not knowing what new thing you are going to try. Find a way to merge them all together! Be willing to fail and try again. Discover your unique way to coax your creativity out of the box others have created for you.

CREATIVITY IS LONGING TO SPEND TIME WITH YOU, TO HELP YOU FIND A REGRET-PROOF LIFE.

As we've seen throughout this whole book, research shows that people who engage with everyday creativity through the five **D.A.N.C.E** habits have higher job satisfaction and performance, salary, better mood, more effective leadership, and are more resilient. Employers who engage their team's creativity have better team cohesion, less employee turnover, higher engagement, improved customer satisfaction and engagement, more innovation, and better financial performance. And with only 18% of employees strongly agreeing that they can take risks at work to be creative, this paradigm shift is low hanging fruit for competitive advantage.

If you dream of what you want to share with the world, it's not creativity — it's imagination. You must actually jump off the end of the virtual plank. Use the tools of risk mitigation and channel your own "BUT WILL YOU DIE?" voice to build your courage to drown out "Todd" and his outdated fears. Feel the cheap carpet with your toes to make sure you have solid ground beneath you before you jump.

REMEMBER TO START SMALL.

With each incremental challenge you conquer, your confidence and willingness to take risks will increase. Have a serious chat with your own version of inner critic Todd, or just give them something to do. Override your outdated survival instinct to see the peril everywhere with your big frontal cortex brain. Jot down some quick ideas now before you lose your nerve.

I would love to be your accountability buddy in your journey to finding your unique contribution, your unique expression or yourself that helps you to find more strength in your voice. Please send me an email or find me on social media and share your attempts — failures welcome. No… encouraged. Creativity is contagious. When I lost the fear of judgement from my vet colleagues and started telling them about my stand-up comedy and my jewelry business, it gave others permission to engage their own unique creative process. Time and time again, colleagues told me about new and rekindled creative pursuits that helped them reclaim some joy in their otherwise stale feeling life. By sharing your joy, you can help others find their creative groove and find a regret-proof life. I hope that my creative project, writing this book, helps you to find that courage to do that thing you want to do. Whether you loved or hated this book, it is my creative heart on my sleeve. I am taking this risk (I won't die if you don't like the book) because, for me, it is better to be the person failing on stage than the person sitting in the audience thinking "I wish I could do that someday."

Post your efforts on social media and tag me on Instagram @artfulscience or Facebook @artfulsciences, even email me (hello@carolinebrookfield.com) some pictures to maintain your momentum. You can even start now by gazing out the window and daydreaming.

If you don't have a window, I've provided a picture of one of my favourite places in the world. I'm not a visual artist but I allow myself to dabble. It's enjoyable, remember? I took one of my own photos and manipulated it in a free online editing program to add artistic effects[37]. It took me about three minutes.

And no, I'm not going to tell you where this picture was taken. Enjoy the ambiguity. It's good for you!

Now…start daydreaming!

---

37 Find out how I edited this photo and the location revealed under Ch. 9 at thereluctantcreative.com/resources

Appendix 𝔸

A Note on Mental Illness

While the stereotypical career creative can be portrayed as a mentally ill, tormented soul full of angst and missing an ear, the reality is different. There are some tenuous links between mental illness and creativity. One study on adopted children from birth mothers with schizophrenia found that schizophrenia-like tendencies in these children allowed for increased creativity so long as they were not expressed as a clinical form of the disorder. A tendency to have some schizophrenia traits is positively correlated with creativity, but that effect is lost in those unfortunately afflicted with full expression of the condition.

ADHD, my own personal neurodivergent blessing, has been implicated in creativity in the literature with mixed results. Recently, a study compared ADHD patients on medication to ADHD patients without medication to a control. The unmedicated ADHD group had higher creativity than the control who had higher creativity than the medicated group. The creativity of those with ADHD might stem from the Dopamine deficiency that characterizes the condition. In a reverse double negative head scratcher (like every single multiple choice question in Psych 101), the brain needs dopamine to turn off the attention switch. It's kind of interesting that a condition with "Attention Deficit" in the name is, in fact, characterized by an overabundance of attention. Walking through the forest? A neurotypical (someone without ADHD) might see a bird. So sweet. Then look! A snake! Yikes! Phew. But what is this beautiful red flower?

Someone with ADHD will hear the centaur singing to his baby, see five species of birds, hear the infuriating sound of you chewing your gum (OMG STOP IT ALREADY), smell the fragrance of the woods, notice the ants building a house in the log, and hear the frogs as they chirp in the swamp, while you happily look at your flower. Those of us with ADHD can get distracted, yes, because you would be too if you could see and hear and feel ALL THE THINGS. For someone without ADHD, the ability to filter incoming information is mediated by dopamine turning ON your filter. Remember the obstacles to creativity? The inner critic and the fear of judgement? With ADHD, those obstacles are napping in the backseat. The inner critic can be crudely compared to executive function, the ability to do "productive stuff" and evaluate information with judgement. Which is not great if your executive function is napping in the backseat during a math test. But when you need to imagine how to learn music from a centaur? Genius. Some research has evaluated this decreased dopamine in the right hemisphere as a precursor to creative thought.

Imagine Jazz musicians playing their instrument in an fMRI, with scientists watching their brain activity. When the musicians played a piece they knew, their executive function was engaged. When asked to improvise, the executive function area was actively inhibited. This inhibition allows for "chaotic cognition" for divergent thinking.

I hope to see a day where the world might learn to adapt and support people with unique talents, instead of making them fit a mold that is convenient for society. If we allow people to explore their unique talents and strengths in the way that works for them (not for others), we might (creatively) solve some of the world's problems. Regardless, mental illness is not a requirement or necessarily helpful in a creative pursuit. If you have feelings of depression or anxiety, or you have questions about neurodiversity please seek professional care and support.

Appendix B

Books, Books, Books!

Throughout this book, I referenced a number of books to read. For ease, I've compiled a list of some of my all-time favourite books for you to dig into and start your own **D.A.N.C.E.** practice. Find the links to all these books at thereluctantcreative.com/resources

Applied Creativity

- *Wreck this Journal, The Line, The Wander Society* — Keri Smith (or any of her books, really)

- *Embrace Your Weird* — Felicia Day

- *The Creativity Challenge* — Tanner Christensen

- *Creativity Rules* — Tina Seelig

- *My Creative Space* — Donald M. Rattner

On Uncertainty

- *Nonsense* — Jamie Holmes

- *The Beauty of Discomfort* — Angela Lang

- *Deviate* — Beau Lotto

Thought-Provoking Creativity

- *War of Art* — Steven Pressfield

- *Imagine* — Jonah Lehrer

- *A Whole New Mind* — Daniel Pink

Other Cool Books

- *In Defense of Troublemakers: The Power of Dissent in Life and Business* — Charlan Nemeth

- *Thinking Fast and Slow* — Daniel Kahnemann

- *Learned Optimism* — Martin Seligman

- *To Sell is Human* — Daniel Pink

- *Drive* — Daniel Pink

Notes

Taking the Creative Leap

Pg. 6:   ...**most either had not found the right activity, or just didn't know what to do.** Ballard, N. (2019, April 30). *Successfully Completing a Creative Project Brings Joy to Nine in Ten Adults.* Retrieved September 2021, from Ipsos: https://www.ipsos.com/en-us/news-polls/Successfully-Completing-a-Creative-Project-Brings-Joy-to-Nine-in-Ten-Adults-Who-Participate-in-Creative-Activities.

Chapter 1: Science Says, "You Are Creative"

Pg. 17:   **2% of adults scoring as "Creative Genius".** Naiman , L. (2014, June 6). *Can Creativity Be Taught.* Retrieved September 2021, from Creativity at Work: https://www.creativityatwork.com/can-creativity-be-taught/.

Pg. 17:   **Dr. Land proposes a solution; decrease the judgement, criticism, and censorship in education, which then also translates to the workplace.** Land, G., & Jarman, B. (1993). *Breaking Point and Beyond.* San Francisco: HarperBusiness.

Pg. 17-18:   ...**believes that creativity needs to be validated by peers in their domain.** Gl veanu, V. P. (2018). Educating which creativity? *Thiking Skills and Creativity, 27,* 25-31. DOI: https://doi.org/10.1016/j.tsc.2017.11.006

Pg. 18:   ...**encouragement for originality, no criticism, and a focus on innovation despite failure.** Witt, L., & Beorkrem, M. N. (1989). Climate for Creative Productivity as a Predictor of Research Usefulness and Organizational Effectiveness in an R&D Organization. *Creativity Research Journal, 2*(1-2), 30-40. DOI: https://doi.org/10.1080/10400418909534298

Pg. 18: **Free flowing ideas, shared knowledge and rewarding innovators adds more depth to the idea of collaboration.** Pulido, S. (2017). Creativity at Work (Publication No. 10801515). Master of Arts Thesis, University of Southern California. *ProQuest Dissertations Publishing.*

Pg. 19: **"Creativity is the person centred process of imagined possibilities and taking embodied expressive action that makes your ideas real."** Burnett, C., & Worwood, M. (2021, April 2). A Scholarly Journey to Redefining Creativity with Marta Ockuly. *The Fueling Creativity Podcast.* https://podcasts.apple.com/us/podcast/a-scholarly-journey-to-redefining-creativity/id1561020163?i=1000515488346.

Pg. 20: **...you can learn techniques to apply to your breathing for a desired outcome, like controlled (box) breathing for anxiety.** Divine, M. (2016, May 4). The Breathing Technique a Navy SEAL Uses to Stay Calm and Focused. *Time.* Retrieved from https://time.com/4316151/breathing-technique-navy-seal-calm-focused/

Pg. 21: **Kids lead with a Zen style "Beginner Mind" because they're life's true beginners.** Kidd, C., & Hayden, B. Y. (2015, November 4). The Psychology and Neuroscience of Curiosity. *Neuron Perspective, 88*(3), 449-460. DOI: https://doi.org/10.1016/j.neuron.2015.09.010.

Pg. 22: **passionately advocates for a stronger role for creativity in education.** Robinson, S. (2006, February). *Do Schools Kill Creativity?* Retrieved from Ted: https://www.ted.com/talks/sir_ken_robinson_do_schools_kill_creativity

Chapter 2: Benefits of D.A.N.C.E.(ing) with Everyday Creativity

Pg. 37: **LinkedIn proclaimed, "Creativity as the number one skill in 2020."** Van Nuys, A. (2019, December 28). *New LinkedIn Research: Upskill Your Employees with the Skills Companies Need Most in 2020.* Retrieved September 2021, from LinkedIn: https://www.linkedin.com/business/learning/blog/learning-and-development/most-in-demand-skills-2020

Pg. 37: **Dell predicted in 2017 that 85% of the jobs in 2030 don't even exist yet.** Institute for the Future for Dell Technologies. (2017). *Emerging Technologies' Impact on Society & Work in 2030.* Institute for the Future for Dell Technologies. Institute for the Future for Dell Technologies.

Pg. 37: **Creative Problem Solving one of the most desired but hardest to find skill sets in 2016.** Levy, F., & Cannon, C. (2016, February 9). *The Bloomberg Job Skills Report 2016: What Recruiters Want.* Retrieved September 2021, from Bloomberg: https://www.bloomberg.com/graphics/2016-job-skills-report/.

Pg. 37: **McKinsey determined that the top missing skills areas are problem solving, critical thinking, innovation, and creativity.** McKinsey & Company. (n.d.). *McKinsey Quarterly.* Retrieved September 2021, from McKinsey &

Company: https://www.mckinsey.com/featured-insights/future-of-work/
five-fifty-soft-skills-for-a-hard-world.

Pg. 37: **...97 million new jobs will be created, with what top required skill?
Analytical thinking and innovation.** World Economic Forum. (2020). *The
Future of Jobs Report 2020.*

Pg. 37-38: **...importance of innovation is recognized by 92% of companies.**
Maddox, T. (2015, May 1). Research: 92 Percent Recognize. *zdnet.*
Retrieved from https://www.zdnet.com/article/research-92-percent-
recognize-importance-of-innovation/.

Pg. 38: **...psychological safety for team members to express creative ideas.**
Somech, A., & Drach-Zahavy, A. (2013, March). Translating Team Creativity
to Innovation Implementation: The Role of Team Composition and Climate
for Innovation. *Journal of Management, 39*(3), 684-708. DOI: https://doi.
org/10.1177/0149206310394187.

Pg. 40: **...benefit of thoughtful and genuine dissent to the bolster better decisions and problem solving.** Nemeth, Charlan J. (2018, March). In Defence
of Troublemakers: The Power of Dissent in Life and Business. New York,
Basic Books.

Pg. 38: **18% of employees feel like they can take risks at work to be creative.**
Wigert, B., & Robison, J. (2018, December 19). Fostering Creativity at
Work: Do Your Managers Push or Crush Innovation? *Gallup.* Retrieved
from https://www.gallup.com/workplace/245498/fostering-creativity-wor
k-managers-push-crush-innovation.aspx.

Pg. 39: **Companies overwhelmingly recognize the importance of innovation.**
Maddox, T. (2015, May 1). Research: 92 percent recognize importance
of innovation. *zdnet.* Retrieved from https://www.zdnet.com/article/
research-92-percent-recognize-importance-of-innovation/.

Pg. 41: **In a Gallup study of more than 16,500 employees, they found three
necessary factors to foster employee creativity.** Wigert, B., & Robison,
J. (2018, December 19). Fostering Creativity at Work: Do Your Managers
Push or Crush Innovation? *Gallup.* Retrieved from https://www.gallup.
com/workplace/245498/fostering-creativity-work-managers-push-crus
h-innovation.aspx.

Pg. 40: **...cultural values and worldviews to reap a benefit of team diversity on
creativity.** Zhou, J., Wang, X. M., Bavato, D., Tasselli, S., & Wu, J. (2019, July).
Understanding the Receiving Side of Creativity: A Multidisciplinary Review
and Implications for Management Research. *Journal of Management, 45*(6),
2570-2595. DOI: 10.1177/0149206319827088.

Pg. 42: **Employees who feel supported to be creative feel like they are doing
their best work and half as likely to say they're looking for another job.**
Shalley, C. E., Zhou, J., & Oldham, G. R. (2004). The Effects of Personal and

Contextual Characteristics on Creativity: Where Should We Go From Here? *Jounral of Management, 30*(6), 933-958. DOI:10.1016/j.jm.2004.06.007.

Pg. 42:   ...**link creativity to business' value, finding a correlation between above average financial performance and a creativity score.** McKinsey & Company. (n.d.). *McKinsey Quarterly.* Retrieved September 2021, from McKinsey & Company: https://www.mckinsey.com/featured-insights/future-of-work/five-fifty-soft-skills-for-a-hard-world.

Pg. 42:   **Creativity among teams has also been shown to increase team cohesion.** Rodríguez-Sánchez, A. M., Devloo, T., Rico, R., Salanova, M., & Anseel, F. (2017). What Makes Creative Teams Tick? Cohesion, Engagement, and Performance Across Creativity Tasks: A Three-Wave Study. *Group & Organization Management, 42*(4), 521-547. DOI: 10.1177/1059601116636476.

Pg. 43:   ...**factors influence how ideas are received, including gender, previous knowledge and experience, perception of creativity, and how "out-of-this-world" the idea is.** Zhou, J., Wang, X. M., Bavato, D., Tasselli, S., & Wu, J. (2019, July). Understanding the Receiving Side of Creativity: A Multidisciplinary Review and Implications for Management Research. *Journal of Management, 45*(6), 2570-2595. DOI: 10.1177/0149206319827088.

Pg. 45:   **Flow, a condition where time seems to stand still.** Csikszentmihalyi, M. (1997). *Finding Flow: The Pyshchology of Engagement with Everyday Life.* New York: Basic Books.

Pg. 45:   ...**found that creativity has a direct effect on increasing positive affect (like happiness) the following day.** Conner, T. S., DeYoung, C. G., & Silvia, P. J. (2016, November 17). Everyday Creative Activity as a Path to Flourishing. *The Journal of Positive Psychology, 13*(2), 181-189.

Pg. 46:   **Kapoor describes four types of "C" creativity seen during COVID.** Kapoor, H., Kaufman J. (2018, December). Meaning-Making Through Creativity During COVID-19. *Frontiers in Psychology,* 11, 36-59. DOI: 10.3389/fpsyg.2020.595990.

Pg. 46:   ...**creative activities generated positive emotions and helped them cope with the negative emotions in response to the pandemic.** Elisondo, Romina Cecilia. (2020). Everyday Creativity in Times of COVID-19: A Qualitative Study from Argentina*. *Creativity. Theories — Research — Applications,* 7:2, 230-250. DOI: 10.2478/ctra-2020-0013.

Pg. 46:   ...**correlation between creativity and positive states.** Binnewies, C., & Wörnlein, S. C. (2011). What Makes a Creative Day? A Diary Study on the Interplay Between Affect, Job Stressors, and Job Control. *Journal of Organizational Behavior, 32*(4), 589-607. Retrieved from https://www.jstor.org/stable/41415688; Han, J., Han, J., & Brass, D. J. (2014). Human Capital Diversity in the Creation of Social Capital for Team Creativity. *Journal of Organizational Behavior, 35*, 54-71. DOI: https://doi.org/10.1002/job.1853

Pg. 46:   ...increase well-being in several groups including nurses. Tuisku, K.,
            Virtanen, M., De Bloom, J., Kinnunen, U. (2016). Cultural Leisure Activities,
            Recovery, and Work Engagement Among Hospital Employees. *Industrial
            Health*, 54, 252-262.

Pg. 46:   ...older students. Cantu, A. G., & Fleuriet, K. J. (2017). "Making the
            Ordinary More Extraordinary": Exploring Creativity as a Health Promotion
            Practice Among Older Adults in a Community-Based Professionally
            Taught Arts Program. *Journal of Holistic Nursing*, 1-11. DOI: https://doi.
            org/10.1177/0898010117697863.

Pg. 46:   ...family caregivers of cancer patients. Walsh, Sandra M. (2004). Testing
            the Efficacy of a Creative-Arts Intervention with Family Caregivers of
            Patients with Cancer. *Journal of Nursing Scholarship*, 36: 214-219. DOI:
            https://doi.org/10.1111/j.1547-5069.2004.04040.x.

Pg. 46:   ...and a wider diversity of individuals in the US. Eschleman, K. J., Madsen,
            J., Alarcon, G., & Barelka, A. (2014). Benefiting from Creative Activity: The
            Positive Relationships Between Creative Activity, Recovery Experiences,
            and Performance-Related Outcomes. *The Journal of Occupational and
            Organizational Psychology*. DOI:10.1111/joop.12064.

Pg. 46-47: University students who expressed creativity had significantly higher
            emotional, psychological and social well-being. Tamannaeifar, M. R.,
            & Motaghedifard, M. (2014, June). Subjective Well-Being and Its Sub-
            Scales Among Students: The Study of Role of Creativity and Self-Efficacy.
            Thinking Skills and Creativity, 12, 37-42. DOI: https://doi.org/10.1016/
            j.tsc.2013.12.003.

Pg. 47:   Knitting in a group significantly improved perceived happiness and so-
            cial connection. Riley, J., Corkhill, B., & Morris, C. (2013). The Benefits of
            Knitting for Personal and Social Wellbeing in Adulthood: Findings from an
            International Survey. *British Journal of Occupational Therapy*, 76(2), 50-57.
            DOI: 10.4276/030802213X13603244419077.

Pg. 47:   New research suggests that we love creativity because we love problem
            solving. Tan, C.S., Tan, S.A., Hashim, I.H.M., Lee, M.N., Wen-Huey Ong,
            A., nor Biniti Yaacob, S. (2019). Problem-Solving Ability and Stress Mediate
            the Relationship Between Creativity and Happiness. *Creativity Research
            Journal*, 31:1, 15-25. DOI: 10.1080/10400419.2019.1568155.

Pg. 47:   85% of them will find a job that has not yet been invented. Institute for
            the Future for Dell Technologies. (2017). *Emerging Technologies' Impact
            on Society & Work in 2030*. Institute for the Future for Dell Technologies.
            Institute for the Future for Dell Technologies.

Pg. 48:   85 million jobs will have been displaced by robots, with 97 million new
            roles to take their place. World Economic Forum. (2020). *The Future of Jobs
            Report 2020*.

Pg. 48: **People who consider themselves creative or engage their creativity "fairly often" have higher job satisfaction.** Banakou, S. (2015, Spring). *Job Satisfaction and Creativity at Work among Greek Employees: The Role of Time Perspective and Financial Crisis.* Linnaeus University, Department of Psychology.

Pg. 48: **...they tend to score up to 30% better on performance ratings.** Eschleman, K. J., Madsen, J., Alarcon, G., & Barelka, A. (2014). Benefiting from Creative Activity: The Positive Relationships Between Creative Activity, Recovery Experiences, and Performance-Related Outcomes. *The Journal of Occupational and Organizational Psychology.* DOI:10.1111/joop.12064.

Pg. 48: **Creative employees were paid 13% more.** Adobe. (2016). *State of Create: 2016.* Adobe.

Pg. 49: **...to retrain or completely change careers to stay in the workforce.** McKinsey & Company. (n.d.). *McKinsey Quarterly.* Retrieved September 2021, from McKinsey & Company: https://www.mckinsey.com/featured-insights/future-of-work/five-fifty-soft-skills-for-a-hard-world.

Pg. 49: **...up to 50% of jobs will require significant reskilling.** RBC. (2018, July). *Humans Wanted: How Canadian Youth Can Thrive in the Age of Disruption.* Retrieved October 2021, from RBC: rbc.com/humanswanted.

Pg. 49: **...92% of job seekers think that now is a good time to look into entering the gig workforce.** Monster. (2020, December). *2021 Hiring Trends: Monster's Predictions for the New Year.* Retrieved October 2021, from Monster: https://hiring.monster.ca/employer-resources/marketing-intelligence/2021-hiring-trends/.

Pg. 50: **...result is a highly collaborative, integrated, and innovative environment.** Brookfield, C. (2021, September). Creative Lifescaping with Steve Rader. *Creative Lifescaping.* Retrieved November 2021, from YouTube: https://www.youtube.com/playlist?list=PL44W3P8iFap3EGAzwRJ8D8D7-3ap04ZkL.

Pg. 53: **"I wish I'd had the courage to live a life true to myself, not the life others expected of me".** Ware, B. (n.d.). *Regrets of the Dying.* Retrieved October 2021, from Bronnie Ware: https://bronnieware.com/blog/regrets-of-the-dying/.

Pg. 55: **...using rationality to derail your advance to creative expression.** Pressfield, S. (2003). *The War of Art: Winning the Inner Creative Battle.* Warner Books.

Pg. 56: **...creativity is showing people what's in your heart and putting that passion into your life and making things.** Brookfield, C. (2021, September). Creative Lifescaping with Brittnay Lyseng. *Creative Lifescaping.* Retrieved November 2021, from YouTube: https://www.youtube.com/watch?v=O-e7X9iRLtHs&list=PL44W3P8iFap3EGAzwRJ8D8D7-3ap04ZkL&index=6.

Chapter 3: Just Tell Me How to Get To Everyday Creativity

Pg. 69: **Employees need to have the room to feel immersed in their work to perform with creativity.** Gevers, Josette M.P., Demerouti, Evangelia. (2011). How Supervisors' Reminders Relate to Subordinates' Absorption and Creativity. *Journal of Managerial Psychology, 28(6), 677-698.* DOI: 10.1108/JPM-09-2011-0055

Pg. 69-70: **Divergent thinking works best in a physical place that feels open, connected with nature, bright, possibly in a blue or green room, furniture with rounded edges, and with many working areas for collaboration like white boards.** Rattner, D. M. (2019). *My Creative Space: How to Design Your Home to Stimulate.* New York, New York: Skyhorse Publishing.

Pg. 70: **...creative ideas fall into three main categories.** Brandt, A., & Eagleman, D. (2018). Under the Hood of Creativity: How the brain bends, breaks and blends existing concepts and objects to invent bold new forms. *Time Special Edition: The Science of Creativity*, pp. 28-35.

Pg. 71: **...blending when he imagined that ultra-strong silk could make an ultra-light bullet proof vest.** BBC News. (2012, January 17). *The Goats with Spider Genes and Silk in Their Milk.* Retrieved October 2021, from BBC News — Science: https://www.bbc.com/news/av/science-environment-16554357.

Pg. 72: **...creativity are the same as techniques to improve comfort, health, and safety.** Dul, J., & Ceylan, C. (2011). Work Environments for Employee Creativity. *Ergonomics, 52*, 12-20.

Pg. 73: **...diversity in the workforce has been shown to increase creativity, leading to increased organizational innovation.** Han, J., Han, J., & Brass, D. J. (2014). Human Capital Diversity in the Creation of Social Capital for Team Creativity. *Journal of Organizational Behavior, 35*, 54-71. DOI: https://doi.org/10.1002/job.1853. Hoever, I. J., van Knippenberg, D., van Ginkel, W. P., & Barkema, H. G. (2012). Fostering Team Creativity: Perspective Taking as Key to Unlocking Diversity's Potential. *Journal of Applied Psychology, 97(5)*, 982-996. DOI: 10.1037/a0029159.

Pg. 73: **Leadership support for creativity, combined with HR creativity initiatives have also been positive drivers of individual creativity in organizations.** Isaksen II, S. G., & Akkermans, H. J. (2011). Creative Climate: A Leadership Lever for Innovation. *Journal of Creative Behavior, 45*, 161-187. https://doi.org/10.1002/j.2162-6057.2011.tb01425.x. Chaubey, A., & Sahoo, C. K. (2019). Role of HR Interventions in Enhancing Employee Creativity and Organizational Innovation: An Empirical Study. *Industrial and Commercial Training, 51(3)*, 195-206. DOI 10.1108/ICT-09-2018-0079.

Pg. 73: **Happier states with a more positive energy are correlated with creativity.** Han, W., Feng, X., Zhang, M., Peng, K., & Zhang, D. (2019, July). Mood States and Everyday Creativity: Employing an Experience Sampling Method and a Day Reconstruction Method. *Frontiers in Psychology, 10*(1698),

1-10. DOI: https://doi.org/10.3389/fpsyg.2019.01698.Silvia, P. J., Beaty, R. E., Nusbaum, E. C., Eddington, K. M., Levin-Aspenson, H., & Kwapil, T. R. (2014). Everyday Creativity in Daily Life: An Experience-Sampling Study of "Little c" Creativity. *Psychology of Aesthetics, Creativity, and the Arts, 8*(2), 183-188. DOI: https://doi.org/10.1037/a0035722.

Pg. 73:   ...certain environmental designs for schools have been proposed to be more conducive to creativity. Hasirci, D., & Demirkan, H. (2007). Understanding the Effects of Cognition in Creative Decision Making: A Creativity Model for Enhancing the Design Studio Process. *reativity Research Journal, 19*(2-3), 2590271. DOI: https://doi.org/10.1080/10400410701397362.

Pg. 73:   ...the most creative states come from a state of ambivalence, where positive and negative states are experienced simultaneously. Fong, C.T. (2006, October). The Effects of Emotional Ambivalence on Creativity. *The Academy of Management Journal, 49*(5), 1016-1030. DOI: https://doi.org/10.5465/amj.2006.22798182.

Pg. 73:   ...students with strong emotional resilience, depression is a catalyst to apply creative thinking to improve their mood and prospects. Wang, Q., Zhao, X., Yuan, Y., & Shi, B. (2021). The Relationship Between Creativity and Intrusive Rumination Among Chinese Teenagers During the COVID-19 Pandemic: Emotional Resilience as a Moderator. *Frontiers in Psychology, 11*, 39-70. DOI: 10.3389/fpsyg.2020.601104.

Pg. 73:   **Environments should allow independent work, be stimulating but not distracting, and allow easy access to resources.** Amabile, T. M., & Pratt, M. G. (2016, November 17). The Dynamic Componential Model of Creativity and Innovation in Organizations: Making progress, Making Meaning. *Research in Organizational Behavior, 36*, 157-183. DOI: https://doi.org/10.1016/j.riob.2016.10.001.

Pg. 73-74:   ...the environment for creativity is what dictates individual creativity. Zhou, J., & Hoever, I. J. (2014). Research on Workplace Creativity: A Review and Redirection. *Annual Review of Organizational Psychology and Organizational Behavior, 1*(1), 333-359. DOI: 10.1146/annurev-orgpsych-031413-091226

Pg. 74:   ...Individual creativity relies on the fundamental condition that we will be safe despite sharing our ideas with the world. Doran, J., & Ryan, G. (2017). The Role of Stimulating Employees' Creativity and Idea Generation in Encouraging Innovation Behaviour in Irish Firms. *Irish Journal of Management, 35*(1), 32-48. DOI:10.1515/ijm-2017-0005.

Pg. 74:   **Circular boardroom desks encouraged discussion and removed the physical hierarchy from meetings to allow more exchange of ideas.** Holt, J. (2014). *Creativity, Inc.: Overcoming the Unseen Forces That Stand in the Way of True Inspiration by Ed Catmull, Amy Wallace... Summarized.* Smashwords Edition.

Pg. 74: **Yet, 70% of people say they would rather create alone.** Adobe. (2016). *State of Create: 2016.* Adobe.

Pg. 75: **32% of employees who could personalize their space were more productive.** Pulido, S. (2017, May). Creativity at Work. *University of Southern California.* ProQuest LLC.

Pg. 75: **Angular furniture can facilitate convergent, more focused thinking.** Wu, Y., Lu, C., Yan, J., Chu, X., Wu, M., & Yang, Z. (2021, Febraury). Rounded or Angular? How the Physical Work Environment in Makerspaces Influences Makers' Creativity. *Journal of Envrionmental Psychology, 72.* DOI: https://doi.org/10.1016/j.jenvp.2020.101546.

Pg. 75: **...support the practice of limiting the visual part of our brain when we are working on an insight or bright idea.** Steidle, A., & Werth, L. (2013, September). Freedom from Constraints: Darkness and Dim Illumination Promote Creativity. *Journal of Environmental Psychology, 35,* 67-80. DOI: https://doi.org/10.1016/j.jenvp.2013.05.003.

Pg. 76: **...narrow, restrictive spaces made people feel confined.** Amabile, T. M., & Pratt, M. G. (2016, November 17). The Dynamic Componential Model of Creativity and Innovation in Organizations: Making Progress, Making Meaning. *Research in Organizational Behavior, 36,* 157-183.. DOI: https://doi.org/10.1016/j.riob.2016.10.001.

Pg. 76: **...*the urge to affiliate with other forms of life.*** Rattner, D. M. (2019). *My Creative Space: How to Design Your Home to Stimulate.* New York, New York: Skyhorse Publishing.

Pg. 77: **...recovery was faster if their view out of the window included trees.** Ulrich, R. S. (1984, April 27). View Through a Window May Influence Recovery from Surgery. *Science, 224*(4647), 420-421. DOI: 10.1126/science.6143402.

Pg. 77: **...research that suggests that a messy desk helps creativity.** Vohs, K. D., Redden, J. P., & Rahinel, R. (2013, August 1). Physical Order Produces Healthy Choices, Generosity, and Conventionality, Whereas Disorder Produces Creativity. *Psychological Science, 24*(9), 1860-1867. DOI: https://doi.org/10.1177/0956797613480186.

Pg. 78: **...orderly desks can also be a good thing, if you are chasing healthy lifestyles, larger donations and status quo solutions.** Vohs, K. D., Redden, J. P., & Rahinel, R. (2013, August 1). Physical Order Produces Healthy Choices, Generosity, and Conventionality, Whereas Disorder Produces Creativity. *Psychological Science, 24*(9), 1860-1867. DOI: https://doi.org/10.1177/0956797613480186.

Pg. 79: **Since cultural views towards colours are so diverse, this could be an effect unique to specific cultures.** Zhu, R., & Mehta, R. (2017). Sensory

Experiences and Consumer Creativity. *Journal of the Association for the Consumer Research, 2*(4), 472-484.

Pg. 79:   **"Any mechanism that can lift us out of our ass-magnets for even a few hours a day has to benefit our health, our brains, and our butts."** Rattner, D. M. (2019). *My Creative Space: How to Design Your Home to Stimulate.* New York, New York: Skyhorse Publishing.

Chapter 4: D. is for Daydream

Pg. 82:   **Dr. Randy Buckner studied the brains of people performing a task-based activity.** Buckner, R.L., Andrews-Hanna, J.R., Schacter, D.L. (2008, April). The Brain's Default Network: Anatomy, Function, and Relevance to Disease. *Annals of the New York Academy of Sciences, 1124,* 1-38. https://doi.org/10.1196/annals.1440.011

Pg. 83:   **It was the "doing nothing" part that ended up being labeled the Default Mode Network.** Raichle, M.E., MacLeod, A.M., Snyder, A.Z., Powers, W.J., Gusnard, D.A., Shulman, G.L. (2001, January). A Default Mode of Brain Function. *Processing of the National Academy of Sciences, 98(2),* 676-6892. DOI: 10.1073/pnas.98.2.676

Pg. 83:   **"an unpleasant, transient affective state in which the individual feels a pervasive lack of interest in and difficulty concentrating on the current activity ... [such that] it takes conscious effort to maintain or return attention to that activity."** Mann, S., & Cadman, R. (2014). Does Being Bored Make Us More Creative? *Creativity Research Journal, 26*(2), 165-173. DOI: 10.1080/10400419.2014.901073.

Pg. 84:   **Boredom results when we can't engage with our environment.** Danckert, J., & Merrifield, C. (2018). Boredom, Sustained Attention and the Default Mode Network. *Experimental Brain Research, 236,* 2507-2518. DOI: https://doi.org/10.1007/s00221-016-4617-5.

Pg. 84:   **Boredom resolves only when we find an activity that is more aligned with our plans and wishes.** Elpidorou, A. (2014, November 3). The Bright Side of Boredom. *Frontiers of Psychology, 5,* 1-4.

Pg. 85:   **They found higher creativity in people who were bored, mainly from a task involving reading (vs. writing).** Mann, S., & Cadman, R. (2014). Does Being Bored Make Us More Creative? *Creativity Research Journal, 26*(2), 165-173. DOI: 10.1080/10400419.2014.901073.

Pg. 85:   **...subjects preferred to self-administer electric shocks to themselves rather than sit alone with their thoughts.** Nederkoorn, C., Vancleef, L., Wilkenhöner, A., Claes, L., & Havermans, R. (2016, March 30). Self-Inflicted Pain Out of Boredom. *Psychiatry Research, 237,* 127-132. DOI: 10.1016/j.psychres.2016.01.063.

Pg. 86:   **A new study links daydreaming to creativity...** Zedelius, C. M., & Schooler, J. W. (2020). Chapter 3 — Capturing the Dynamics of Creative Daydreaming. *Creativity and the Wandering Mind*, 55-72.

Pg. 87:   **During an undemanding task, we keep our analytical brain just busy enough to allow our minds to wander, leading to more creative ideas.** Baird, B., Smallwood, J., Mrazek, M. D., Kam, J. W., Franklin, M. S., & Schooler, J. W. (2012). Inspired by Distraction: Mind Wandering Facilitates Creative Incubation. *Psychological Science, 23*(10), 1117-1122. DOI: https://doi.org/10.1177/0956797612446024.

Pg. 88:   **Mindfulness is the practice of being completely in the moment, not dreaming about possibilities...** Zedelius, C. M., & Schooler, J. W. (2015). Mind Wandering "Ahas" Versus Mindful Reasoning: Alternative Routes to Creative Solutions. *Frontiers in Pyschology, 6*(834). DOI: 10.3389/fpsyg.2015.00834.

Pg. 88:   **...that mindfulness can calm our instinctive negative response to change, disruption, or ambiguity.** Fewster, K., & O'Connor, P. (2017, May). Embracing Ambiguity in the Workplace. *Change2020*, 1-15.

Pg. 88:   **...mind wandering is associated with a lower mood.** Baird, B., Smallwood, J., Mrazek, M. D., Kam, J. W., Franklin, M. S., & Schooler, J. W. (2012). Inspired by Distraction: Mind Wandering Facilitates Creative Incubation. *Psychological Science, 23*(10), 1117-1122. DOI: https://doi.org/10.1177/0956797612446024.

Chapter 5: A. is for Ambiguity

Pg. 97:   **In one study, two groups were each shown a set of playing cards.** Holmes, J. (2015). *Nonsense: The Power of Not Knowing.* New York: Crown Publishing Group.

Pg. 101:   **...it seemed that the group had been getting ready to turn themselves in.** Holmes, J. (2015). *Nonsense: The Power of Not Knowing.* New York: Crown Publishing Group.

Pg. 101-102: **...TOA correlated highly with resilience and creativity.** Fewster, K., & O'Connor, P. (2017, May). Embracing Ambiguity in the Workplace. *Change2020*, 1-15.

Pg. 102:   **Having a high TOA is correlated to a wide array of benefits to both the individual and the organization.** Fewster, K., & O'Connor, P. (2017, May). Embracing Ambiguity in the Workplace. *Change2020*, 1-15.

Pg. 103:   **...a systematic review of many studies determined that TOA is associated with psychological well-being.** Hancock, J., & Mattick, K. (2020). Tolerance of Ambiguity and Psychological Well-Being in Medical Training: A Systematic Review. *Medical Education, 54*, 125-137. DOI: 10.1111/medu.14031.

Pg. 103: Those with a high need for closure, low TOA, and years in practice were significantly predicted to suffer from work-related stress. Iannello, P., Mottini, A., Tirelli, S., Riva, S., & Antonietti, A. (2017). Ambiguity and Uncertainty Tolerance, Need for Cognition, and Their Association with Stress. A Study Among Italian Practicing Physicians. *Medical Education Online, 22*(1). https://doi.org/10.1080/10872981.2016.1270009.

Pg. 104: Curiosity is a corrective factor for physicians with both high and low tolerance of ambiguity to make better decisions. Reis-Dennis, S., Gerrity, M. S., & Geller, G. (2020). Tolerance for Uncertainty and Professional Development: a Normative Analysis. *J Genl Intern Med., 36*(8), 2408-2413.

Pg. 104: Medical students who participated in an art appreciation course had higher TOA. Bentwich, M. E., & Gilbey, P. (2017). More Than Visual Literacy: Art and the Enhancement of Tolerance for Ambiguity and Empathy. *BMC Medical Education, 17*(200). DOI 10.1186/s12909-017-1028-7.

Pg. 104-105: ...a six-week program focused on learning and discussion around uncertainty vs control resulted in increased TOA... Molton, I. R., Koelmel, E., Curran, M., von Geldern, G., Ordway, A., & Alschuler, K. N. (2019). Pilot Intervention to Promote Tolerance for Uncertainty in Early Multiple Sclerosis. *Rehabilitaion Psychology, 64*(3), 339-350. DOI: https://doi.org/10.1037/rep0000275.

Pg. 105: ...successfully introduced a knowledge management model that resulted in both increased TOA as well as productivity... Tsirikas, A. N., Katsaros, K. K., & Nicolaidis, C. S. (2012). Knowledge Management, Tolerance of Ambiguity and Productivity. *Employee Relations, 34*(4), 344-359. DOI 10.1108/01425451211236814.

Pg. 112: ...to determine what factors might help employees and leaders with uncertainty. Fewster, K., & O'Connor, P. (2017, May). Embracing Ambiguity in the Workplace. *Change2020*, 1-15.

Chapter 6: N. is for Novelty

Pg. 113: The act of trying new things, forcing our brain to adapt to writing with the wrong hand, or tackling something in a new way, keeps our brain growing and making new connections. Eagleman , D. (2020). *Livewired: The Inside Story of the Ever-Changing Brain*. Pantheon Books.

Pg. 114: Seeking novelty expands our universe-brain to allow more connections between concepts. Ramsden, K. (2018). *Success Hangover: Ignite your NextAact. Screw Your Status Quo. Feel Alive Again*. Lionscrest Publishing.

Pg. 122: ...as bilingualism has been proven to make you more creative. Ricciardelli, L. A. (1992). Creativity and Bilingualism. *The Journal of Creative Behavior, 26*(4), 242-254. DOI: https://doi.org/10.1002/j.2162-6057.1992.tb01183.x.

Chapter 7: C. is for Curiosity

Pg. 128:   ...have been new questions about the relevance and validity of the original work cited in the Dunning-Kruger effect. Jarry, J. (2020, Decembver 17). *The Dunning-Kruger Effect Is Probably Not Real.* Retrieved October 2021, from McGill Office for Science and Society : https://www.mcgill.ca/oss/article/critical-thinking/dunning-kruger-effect-probably-not-real.

Pg. 130:   ...two main types of curiosity... Hardy III, J. H., Ness, A. M., & Mecca, J. (2016). Outside the Box: Epistemic Curiosity as a Predictor of Creative Problem Solving and Creative Performance. *Personality and Individual Differences, 104,* 230-237. DOI: https://doi.org/10.1016/j.paid.2016.08.004.

Pg. 131:   ...curiosity positively predicts creative performance. Hardy III, J. H., Ness, A. M., & Mecca, J. (2016). Outside the Box: Epistemic Curiosity as a Predictor of Creative Problem Solving and Creative Performance. *Personality and Individual Differences, 104,* 230-237. DOI: https://doi.org/10.1016/j.paid.2016.08.004.

Pg. 132:   ...curiosity helps creativity through a concept called "idea linking." Hagtvedt, L. P., Dossinger, K., Harrison, S. H., & Huang, L. (2019). Curiosity Made the Cat More Creative: Specific Curiosity as a Driver of Creativity. *Organizational Behavior and Human Decision Processes, 150,* 1-13. DOI: https://doi.org/10.1016/j.obhdp.2018.10.007.

Pg. 133:   **Curiosity also requires autonomy, responsibility, and freedom...** Merck KGaA. (2020). *State of Curiosity Report 2020 — Our Company Results.* Germany: emdgroup.

Pg. 133:   **Steve Jobs and Walt Disney have credited curiosity for their creative output.** Hardy III, J. H., Ness, A. M., & Mecca, J. (2016). Outside the Box: Epistemic Curiosity as a Predictor of Creative Problem Solving and Creative Performance. *Personality and Individual Differences, 104,* 230-237. DOI: https://doi.org/10.1016/j.paid.2016.08.004.

Pg. 133:   **Dr. Diane Hamilton calls curiosity the "one of the most critical determinants of performance."** Hamilton, D. (2020, April). How to Instill Curiosity in the Workplace. *Forbes Coaches Council.* Retrieved November 2021 from Forbes: https://www.forbes.com/sites/forbescoachescouncil/2020/04/03/how-to-instill-curiosity-in-the-workplace/?sh=6e7463de42e2.

Pg. 133:   **50% or more of employees are predicted to require a job change or significant reskilling.** RBC. (2018, July). *Humans Wanted: How Canadian youth can thrive in the age of disruption.* Retrieved October 2021, from RBC: rbc.com/humanswanted.

Pg. 134:   **Intellectual humility is driven by truth-seeking...** Silvia, P. J., Beaty, R. E., Nusbaum, E. C., Eddington, K. M., Levin-Aspenson, H., & Kwapil, T. R. (2014). Everyday Creativity in Daily Life: An Experience-Sampling Study of "Little c" Creativity. *Psychology of Aesthetics, Creativity, and* *the Arts, 8*(2), 183-188. DOI: 10.1037/a0035722; Leary, M. R., Diebels, K. J., Davisson, E., Jongman-Sereno, K. P., Isherwood, J. C., Raimi, K. T., Hoyle, R. H. (2017). Cognitive and Interpersonal Features of Intellectual Humility. *Personality and Social Psychology Bulletin, 43*(6), 793-813. DOI: 10.1177/0146167217697695.

Pg. 134: **Research is now revealing that if we can sit comfortably in an ambivalent state, and accept ambiguity with more equanimity, we will increase our creative potential.** Henriksen D, Richardson C, Shack K. Mindfulness and creativity: Implications for thinking and learning. *Think Skills Creat.* 2020;37:100689. DOI:10.1016/j.tsc.2020.100689.

Pg. 133: **A curious workplace has fewer decision-making errors, more innovation, less group conflict, and better team performance (through communication).** Gino, F. (2018). The Business Case for Curiosity. *Harvard Business Review* (September — October), 48-57.

Pg. 136: **Curiosity can improve mental well-being,** Gallagher, M.W., Lopez, S.J. (2007, October). Curiosity and Well-Being. *The Journal of Positive Psychology, 2(4),* 236-248. doi.org/10.1080/17439760701552345.

Pg. 136: *...being curious makes life way more fun.* Swan, G. E., & Carmelli, D. (1996). Curiosity and Mortality in Aging Adults: A 5-Year Follow-Up of the Western Collaborative Group Study. *Psychology and Aging, 11*(3), 449-453.

Chapter 8: E. is for Edit Later

Pg. 143: **...nor a massive rejection filter to consider how their ideas might change others' perceptions of them.** Kidd, C., & Hayden, B. Y. (2015, November 4). The Psychology and Neuroscience of Curiosity. *Neuron Perspective, 88*(3), 449-460.

Pg. 147: **...one a team of business school students, the other...kindergartners.** Skillman, P. (2019, April 14). *Peter Skillman: The Design Challenge (also called Spaghetti Tower).* Retrieved October 2021, from Medium: https://medium.com/@peterskillman/the-design-challenge-also-called-spaghetti-tower-cda62685e15b.

Chapter 9: Will You D.A.N.C.E. With Me?

Pg. 154: **...25% of Americans who don't engage their creativity.** Ballard, N. (2019, April 30). *Successfully Completing a Creative Project Brings Joy to Nine in Ten Adults.* Retrieved September 2021, from Ipsos: https://www.ipsos.com/en-us/news-polls/Successfully-Completing-a-Creative-Project-Brings-Joy-to-Nine-in-Ten-Adults-Who-Participate-in-Creative-Activities

Pg. 157: **To keep your mind sharp and working optimally, we need to challenge it a little bit every day.** Eagleman , D. (2020). *Livewired: The Inside Story of the Ever-Changing Brain.* Pantheon Books.

Pg. 162: **...18% of employees strongly agreeing that they can take risks at work to be creative, this paradigm shift is low hanging fruit for competitive advantage.** Wigert, B., & Robison, J. (2018, December 19). Fostering Creativity at Work: Do Your Managers Push or Crush Innovation? *Gallup.* Retrieved from: https://www.gallup.com/workplace/245498/fostering-creativity-work-managers-push-crush-innovation.aspx.

Appendix A

Pg. 165: **...that effect is lost in those unfortunately afflicted with full expression of the condition.** Acar, S., Chen, X., & Cayirdag, N. (2018, May). Schizophrenia and Creativity: A Meta-analytic Review. *ScienceDirect, 195,* 23-31. Retrieved from https://doi.org/10.1016/j.schres.2017.08.036.

Pg. 166: **...unmedicated ADHD group had higher creativity than the control who had higher creativity than the medicated group.** White, H. A. (2018, September 30). Thinking "Outside the Box": Unconstrained Creative Generation in Adults with Attention Deficit Hyperactivity Disorder. *Journal of Creative Behavior, 54,* 472-483. DOI: https://doi.org/10.1002/jocb.382.

Pg. 167: **Some research has evaluated this decreased dopamine in the right hemisphere as a precursor to creative thought.** Aberg, K. C., Doell, K. C., & Schwartz, S. (2017, October). The "Creative Right Brain" Revisited: Individual Creativity and Associative Priming in the Right Hemisphere Relate to Hemispheric Asymmetries in Reward Brain Function. *Cerebral Cortex, 27,* 4946-4959. DOI: 10.1093/cercor/bhw288.

Pg. 167: **...inhibition allows for "chaotic cognition" for divergent thinking.** White, H. A. (2018, September 30). Thinking "Outside the Box": Unconstrained Creative Generation in Adults with Attention Deficit Hyperactivity Disorder. *Journal of Creative Behavior, 54,* 472-483. DOI: https://doi.org/10.1002/jocb.382.

Acknowledgments

This is the part of the book where I say thanks to everyone who helped me write the book. Don't take this the wrong way, but first I'm going to thank myself. Because this was hard. Writing a book is hard, and we often forget to thank ourselves for putting in the effort to make something happen, and have the courage to share a piece of ourselves with the world. I would love it if you would acknowledge whatever you did to expand your comfort zone throughout this book. GO THANK YOURSELF. No, read it again. GO *THANK YOURSELF!*

Now, having said that, I do have some other people to thank. My husband, Ken who perhaps dubiously supports my random projects. There is a reason my family calls him long-suffering Ken. Although he does not always understand what I'm doing, he uses creativity to support me by making meals and by finding ways to balance the household duties and budget. I want to thank my sons Liam and Cole for keeping me humble, and for showing me how to be courageous every day. High School and Junior High are not easy, yet they show up every day with honesty and enthusiasm. They will be embarrassed that I called them out (secretly, they love it...I think). Luckily, I might never convince them to read the book.

I would also like to thank my parents, Mike and Kate, for showing me that even though it's hard to show up without a mask to blend into society, it makes you way more interesting.

This book, my speaking career, and my foray into stand up comedy might not have happened without the firm shove from Kelsey Ramsden. While Kelsey has moved on from coaching (at least that is what she told me), the few years I worked with her changed my life. From artwork at a vineyard, leaping off a dock, meditations with sniper rifles, to deep explorations of intuition, Kelsey showed me how to find my own way forward. She is a true provocateur and the most intuitive person I know. Thanks also to Kelsey for the introduction to Courtney Lochner. Courtney is a gifted editor and the first person to set eyes on my first draft. Thanks for making it so much better.

Thanks to my incredible production team who helped me get through the painstaking minutia of writing a book. To my quirky and competent reference-annihilating editor, Lindsay Harle @quirkylindsayharle, and my delightful and artistically gifted formatter Elena Reznikova. An extra special glitter bomb of thanks to Alexis Kelly @arkwriting, my marketing student who kept me on track by holding me accountable for deadlines, creating beautiful social media posts with amazing copy, as well as laughing off my ADHD distractibility and disorderliness. Thanks to the Canada Summer Jobs Program for providing funding for me to hire Alexis. Oh Canada!

Extra thank yous to a few random influential folks in my life. Stu Hughes, who launched me headfirst into stand up comedy with a wedgie, and Mme Small (my grade two teacher) for accepting me for who I am and showing me that I can be myself and be ok.

I was one of the extremely fortunate creative geniuses in a Guelph preschool to be guided by another creative genius, author Robert Munsch. "Munschy baby," as I called him, was probably sprinkling creative stars around my universe brain, and telling me that I was totally okay just the way I was, at a time when I needed it the most.

Finally, thank you to all my beta readers who helped to brainstorm titles, give criticism of the book in its early stages, and provide support for this journey. Too many people to name here, you know who you are. I'm sure I am forgetting someone important, and for that transgression I also say, "thank you." And, *GO THANK YOURSELF.* You deserve it!

About the Author

Caroline is a speaker, veterinarian, entrepreneur, mom, stand up comic and author. She believes that if everyone took tiny unconventional actions every day to expand their comfort zone, we would change the world.

Caroline received her D.V.M with honours from the Ontario Veterinary College. She is a certified level 2 Creative Problem Solving facilitator, and holds a Certificate of Professional Management from the University of Calgary.

Caroline plays in the Rocky Mountains near her home in Calgary, Alberta, that she shares with her long suffering husband, her brilliant teenage boys, a lazy rescue dog, and two cockatiels. Her lectures go unheeded by her family. The dog listens, sometimes.

This is why Caroline loves to speak from small and large stages to audiences of Reluctant Creatives, to mobilize human ingenuity and activate enthusiasm. She is known for her light and funny style, deeply rooted in data. On stage, Caroline uses the performance mullet approach: fun up top, data in the back. If you are looking for an energizing keynote or workshop to improve job performance, engagement, and collaboration in your group or organization full of Reluctant Creatives, email Caroline at **hello@carolinebrookfield.com.**

You can read more about Caroline on her website,

www.carolinebrookfield.com

If you need a boost getting started, check out the video dares and more resources at **thereluctantcreative.com/resources**

You can also download the activities on this page to email and share with a friend. Sharing is caring, and creativity is contagious.

On this page, explore dozens of interviews with reluctant creatives who explore how everyday creativity has helped them to become better humans, at home and at work. Steal their hacks and improve your life. They didn't read the fine print.

https://www.facebook.com/artfulsciences
https://www.linkedin.com/in/caroline-brookfield
Youtube: https://bit.ly/3y3DZpF
www.instagram.com/artfulscience

THANKS
FOR READING THIS
LITERARY MULLET —
FUN IN THE FRONT,
DATA IN THE BACK.

IF YOU ENJOYED THIS BOOK,
PLEASE CONSIDER LEAVING
AN HONEST REVIEW ON AMAZON,
GOODREADS, OR YOUR FAVORITE
STORE. AND PLEASE SHARE
WITH A FRIEND!

—Caroline

Manufactured by Amazon.ca
Bolton, ON